Dad's War

Dad's War

by

Don Moggs

The Pentland Press Limited
Edinburgh · Cambridge · Durham

First published in 1994 by
The Pentland Press Ltd.
1 Hutton Close
South Church
Bishop Auckland
Durham

ISBN 1 85821 160 3

Typeset by Elite Typesetting Techniques, Southampton.
Printed and bound by Antony Rowe Ltd., Chippenham.

To my sons, Stephen and David

Contents

Chapter	1	Introduction	1
	2	The Drums Sound	4
	3	The Phoney War	6
	4	The Blitz	14
	5	The Long Wait	26
	6	The Call to Arms	39
	7	Shipped Overseas	50
	8	Go West Young Man	55
	9	EFTS at Neepawa	59
	10	Service Flying Training School	74
	11	Graduation	125
	12	Now you are a Pilot and leave in New York	130
	13	GR on Prince Edward Island	139
	14	New York again (What More Leave!)	142
	15	Moncton and Home	146
	16	The Wedding or The Rocket	153
	17	Awaiting a Posting	157
	18	Overseas again	161
	19	VE Day! In Jerusalem and VE Day at Home	169
	20	Battle Courses and Football	178
	21	Administration and Accountancy	185
	22	Demobilisation	194
	23	Conclusion	196
Appendix		Old Friends	198

Chapter 1

Introduction

No matter how hard one tries to understand what really happened the young can never quite comprehend what it was really like. My dad knew a little of what his dad did in the First World War and could repeat some of the stories he remembered, but when it came down to it it amounted to precious little when one considered the length of time my grandad had spent as a soldier fighting in the trenches. Grandad it seems volunteered in August 1914 and was in France later that year as a sergeant in the 11th Battalion Royal Fusiliers. He was at all the familiar names of that terrible War – Ypres (or as he called it Wipers), Arras, Somme, etc., and Dad told me what he could remember from his father. There was the time when Grandad was trying to make his way back to base under a heavy bombardment when tearing along the track came four horses towing a gun carriage, and the rider slowed as he got up with Dad and yelled at him to jump up, which Grandad did, and then much to his surprise saw that the young rider who had 'rescued' him was his young brother, Vic, who was only sixteen. Later in the war Dad said Uncle Vic was taken prisoner and said his life was saved by a German doctor. Then there was the very sad story of how Grandad's father asked Grandad, the eldest, to look after his other brother, Eddy, who had just joined the same regiment. Grandad managed to get him transferred to his Company but shortly afterwards Eddy was killed when he volunteered for a wiring party. There were one or two other stories but Dad never quite remembered the details. It wasn't all fighting however, Grandad did get some leave and on one of these leaves he married Grandmother in the village church in Forty Hill, north of Enfield, the latter now a London borough. Dad said his mother often told the story about the wedding and how the best man, an old friend of Grandad who had joined with him, had made them laugh. The best man

was still a private whilst Grandad was a sergeant. The vicar remarked that
Grandad was very young to have sergeant's stripes, when the best man
chirped in, 'They chuck 'em away in our mob.'

'Then why haven't you got any?' retorted the vicar, who had just told
them his name was Onions and that of course he had been called Stinker at
school.

'I can't catch!' came the reply.

Then there was that story of how Grandad's father lost his gold pocket
watch in a lift in the West End when taking Grandad and Grandma to a
theatre whilst Grandad was on leave from the front. It seems that when
Grandad got back to France he related the story to some fellow soldiers
and one of them who was about to get his seven days leave admitted that
by profession he was a pick-pocket and reckoned that he might be able to
recover the watch. A week later he returned from leave but although he
said he had traced the man who worked that particular area of the West
End he was too late to save the watch from the melting pot.

The above is almost the sum total of what Dad remembered of what his
dad had told him about the First World War. Dad still had the framed
certificate his father had been given after he had been Mentioned in
Despatches; there it was on the wall of his study – 'For distinguished and
gallant services in the Field . . .' it says and is signed by Winston
Churchill – Secretary of State for War.

Well what is all this to do with my dad's war I hear you say – nothing
except to illustrate that, although most things told about wars are concerned with the fighting, occasionally things are said that make the young
sit up and say, half a minute perhaps there was something else going on
besides the wounding and killing. After all life went on and, although war
does mean change, it affects some more than others.

So as there were theatres open in the First World War there were probably theatres open in my dad's war, I thought, and I remembered how he
had told me when I was very young that people were not always shooting in
a war. It was difficult for me to understand then but when later one of our
masters at school told us about Douglas Bader and I talked to my dad who
explained that the Battle of Britain, as important as it was, only represented
about three months of a six-year war, I began to see a lot must have happened elsewhere and to many others. I resolved then to question him more
fully and if possible to record what I had been told. It turned out to be quite
different from what I had imagined, but then this is only my dad's story.

The tale I tell is of a young man who was seventeen when war was
declared, an ordinary young man with hopes the same as others. He knew

in his heart since the Munich crisis that time was running out for many of the young and, although it never bothered him, it influenced his attitude to work. He had been advised to study by the man who had helped him get a position in the Metropolitan Water Board but he did not start and used the coming war as an excuse. It became a period of waiting and surviving. He lived through the London Blitz and later served with the RAF. It is not a story of gallantry, but one which will remind some and perhaps help others understand what it was like to be young half a century ago.

Chapter 2

The Drums Sound

Fifty years is a long time to remember back and therefore some things may be in the wrong order but certainly from 1941 onwards I was able to make some checks against the scores of letters written between Dad and my brother Stephen's Mum. I believe that all letters received by both parties right up until the end of 1946 have been kept and, although we know these to be letters showing affection, they do give a guide as to what happened.

The first thing I can remember being told in relation to the War in fact happened one year before war started and as Dad says he has never heard anyone mention it since he believed it to not be generally known.

In the Summer of 1938 Dad was in the sixth form at Enfield Grammar School. He was not there taking a special course but, although 'studying' a good deal, including Commercial French, Spanish, Typewriting, Shorthand, and Ballroom Dancing (this I understand was not in the school syllabus but the boys taught themselves in spare time from Victor Sylvester's book), he was actually waiting to find a job. At first it did not seem as if it would be a problem as he had a good Matric and was both House and School Football Captain. However, this was the thirties and jobs were not easy to get. He had written to many banks and insurance companies but never was asked to an interview. Something would turn up he thought but in the meanwhile there was nothing to do but wait. Although he tried hard he admitted to me that he was enjoying school probably for the first time in his life, and with thoughts of war in mind a future career was less pressing, he just needed a job (a job with a pension his dad had said) to earn some money and help his mum and dad who had kept him at school for so long. It seems strange now but probably 90 per cent of children left school at fourteen in those days and here was Dad sixteen and still at school!

4

Adolph Hitler at this time had made another demand to enlarge Germany and it seemed inevitable that this would be the start of war. So close was it that sixth form boys were asked if they would volunteer to work in the evenings in a factory to assemble gas marks. There was no pay but Dad and a few friends joined in and were sent to a factory in the Queensway, Ponders End, an industrial part of Enfield.

The work was quite straightforward. They had to join the rubber face-piece to a canister by means of an inch-wide elastic band. Then having completed the simple assembly put these into cardboard boxes for issue to the public.

As history tells us, war was averted at that time when Neville Chamberlain went to Munich to see Hitler and got him to sign a piece of paper in which Hitler said he had no other territorial claims after the present one was settled.

Most people seemed to believe war had really gone away. However, there were some who were not so easily convinced and when the Headmaster at his school organised a Thanksgiving service for peace, Dad and a handful of his friends refused to go. Each one was called before the Head and asked to give his reason for not attending, and none was punished when they said they did not believe war had been averted. The Headmaster, L.C. Soar, no doubt secretly was on their side – and how right they were was soon to be revealed. Dad says half of those lads were later killed in the RAF.

Chapter 3

The Phoney War

The story of how war did eventually come has been told many times and Dad's account is very little different from what has been said before. Dad told me what he remembered and happened to him on that fateful day.

It was a year after the Munich Crisis and Germany had just invaded Poland. Both Britain and France had given ultimatums to them to stop the invasion or else a state of war would exist. The warning was ignored and thus on Sunday morning, 3 September 1939, the Prime Minister talked on the radio to the British people and said we were at war with Germany.

Dad had listened to the broadcast with his parents and his young cousin who had come round home to go out with Dad for a Sunday morning walk. They started out on the walk but did not get far when the air-raid siren sounded – they immediately turned around and went back home to collect gas masks and see what would happen. Nothing happened and shortly the all clear sounded. Whether they continued the walk I never discovered but I remember Dad saying that after this initial scare very little happened over the next several months in a period which later became known as the phoney war. Of course the British Expeditionary Force went across to France and with the French behind what they thought was their impregnable Maginot Line and the Germans on the Seigfried Line, all, for the time being, was quiet.

It seems that by the start of the War Dad had been at work some months having found a job through Grandad talking to the rent collector of the house in which they lived. He had started soon after Munich with the Metropolitan Water Board and travelled by steam train and bus up to New River Head in Islington – 'All except the first day!' Dad said. Jobs were very hard to get in the thirties and Dad was keen not to be late on his first day at work and accordingly left early catching the train to Stoke

6

Newington – when he got off the station he found he was so early that he decided to start walking. He was not too familiar with the bus route but once he came to the one remaining tramline in North London, which went from the Manor House through the Kingsway Tunnel to the Embankment and then over the river to South London, he knew he was on the right road. He ended up walking the whole way – nearly four miles – and met the one other new boy on arrival. Dad said the other boy had pinstripe trousers, a black jacket, an umbrella and a bowler hat – whilst Dad was wearing his one and only suit from the Fifty Shilling Tailors. 'You can imagine how I felt,' Dad said. Dad ended this brief memory by adding that the poor lad was killed during the War. 'So was old Henry,' Dad said, 'the lad who was assigned to teach me the ropes on my first days at work.'

I later came to understand and appreciate Dad's habit of interrupting the main story with these little episodes which helped me understand the life and times of half a century ago. But back to the War.

As soon as war was declared all places of entertainment were closed; that meant cinemas, theatres, dance halls. Dad says no one knew what to expect and having been issued with gas masks months earlier, everyone thought London to be an immediate target. As far as Dad remembers all football was initially stopped and the Football League later devised leagues by areas to avoid unnecessary travel. The big amateur clubs were also affected and reserve team games were for a time limited. Dad was a keen footballer and had been playing for his Old Boys and then for his new employers in the Nemean and Southern Amateur leagues – the Water Board ran four sides going under the name Aquarius, and in a matter of months played for all four sides, starting off in the fourth and ending up with games in the first. Then just before the '39/40 season was due to start he was offered a trial for Enfield Town, then in the Athenian League. The trial took place, according to the newspaper cutting he showed me, ex- actly one week before war was declared.

Of course football must have been far from his mind when war was declared but he told me that when things settled down he was able to play again but many clubs were not running reserve sides to start with and this, he seems to remember, was the position with many of the big amateur clubs. To play for Aquarius meant much travel south of the river which was almost like a foreign country to Dad. I asked what he meant. He said it seemed quite different from North London – there were still crowds of trams unlike North London which had changed to trolley-buses some years earlier, and there were few underground stations and the local train services were electric instead of steam. The people living in South

Dad's War

ENFIELD FOOTBALL CLUB

Hon. Res. Team Sec.:

J. H. GAYLER,

Phone Nos.:

Enfield 2139. National 5295

(Business Hours)

119 LADYSMITH RD.,

ENFIELD, MIDDX.

Dear Sir,

You have been selected to play in the following ~~match~~ *trial. Kindly notify me by return if you are unable to do so.*

Yours faithfully,

J. H. GAYLER.

Date *Wed Aug 23rd*

Opponents

Ground *Stadium Enfield*

Competition

Kick-off *6.15 Sharp*

~~Travelling Arrangements~~ *Kindly bring full Kit include White Shirt*

Trial at Enfield FC on 23 August 1939. War declared 3 September 1939.

London no doubt felt the same difference when they travelled to where he lived, he said.

About this time Dad was transferred from Head Office to a new local office in the High Road in Tottenham and, instead of having to travel by bus and train, started to use his bicycle, which had been a present on his twelfth birthday and cost his parents £4 15*s*. – two weeks' wages for some men at the time.

After a week or so of war with nothing happening, the cinemas and dance halls re-opened their doors and life once more became normal – or as normal as it could be with a war in the background.

So life went on much the same as before war was declared; Dad in the evenings met up with friends in the snooker hall above Burtons (the Spot Club) and then they would go on to a dance or a cinema, but he did try to stay home one night a week. Sometimes his friends would come round home and play cards or Monopoly with the family – yes, I was surprised they had that game. Dad says it was expensive to buy and cost his parents ten shillings.

The lads also had a few dancing lessons at a Firs Hall in Winchmore Hill where the old male teacher enjoyed teaching not only the then current ballroom dancing but also those of yesteryear such as the Lancers. It helped to be able to dance in those days and Dad's sister, my Auntie Babs, helped him a lot as she had even at that time won several competitions. Dancing in the working-class areas of London and its suburbs was of a high standard and if you wanted to meet the opposite sex this was the best way, and those who couldn't dance were less popular.

Thus time passed and Christmas 1939 came and went, and Dad became eighteen and entitled to his first holiday from work. It was now over a year since he had first entered the great Revenue Hall at New River Head near the Angel at Islington, but so much had happened in that first year that to the young man it seemed much longer. His stay at Head Office sitting on high stools in a vast office, known as the Revenue Hall, had not lasted more than a few months but he said he had been most pleased to be transferred to a new small and, what turned out to be, most friendly, office in Tottenham – a short walk from the Spurs ground, his team from a very young age. The office was fitted out with new furniture but still with high stools.

He was of course the junior at the office and thus took a fair share of the less dignified jobs which were expected of the young in those days. There was no central heating and the main office, seating about seven persons, was heated by an open fire and one of Dad's jobs was to buy firelighters and hump coal. At this point when relating this part of his story he frequently smiled when remembering what must have been quite a happy time. He told me of how his under-boss nearly set the office on fire when he decided the chimney needed sweeping. It was apparently not unusual to burn a chimney out to save having the sweep but Dad sensed that old Charlie Moore liked a good fire up the chimney. On this one occasion it really got going and the single story building in which they were shook so much that you couldn't easily stay on your stool. Fortunately it did burn itself out but it was a big laugh at the time.

Apart from the fire duties, often taken over by someone else, he could be sent out to buy a tuppenny or fourpenny bar of chocolate for one of his seniors, and of course he usually ended up with a square for himself. He said he resolved that when he earned more money he too would buy himself a bar, but for the time being he had other uses for the money which was left after paying his mum and dad for his keep.

Dad liked music and had bought himself a record player (39s. 6d.). He still has nearly all of his original 48s from that time, a mixture of Bing Crosby, Kate Smith, and operatic arias! He also has a Tommy Dorsey record with an unnamed singer on the label who he says is Frank Sinatra. He told me that the tunes of 'Roll out the Barrel', and 'We're going to hang out the washing on the Siegfried Line', were not at all popular with the young, and why they have survived as typical of the tunes of the early part of the war he says he can't imagine – they were a big laugh to the young who thought them to be corny and he says he squirms every time he hears them sung as being typical. 'We had more taste than that,' he said.

After working for over a year Dad had become entitled to a paid holiday of one week but of course since he was a junior he had little choice as to when he could take it; thus it came about that Dad's first summer holiday had to be taken in April. His friend Bob was in much the same position as junior in the Potters Bar branch of the Westminster Bank and the two of them arranged to take their holidays at the same time. They were both at peak fitness, regularly playing football (it was Bob who had gone with him when they were invited for trials) and cycling a great deal. They decided to cycle down to Devon. Both had to go to work on the Saturday morning, the holiday starting in the afternoon and thus they left Enfield in the early afternoon and cycled through North and West London, and down the A30 to Basingstoke where they arrived early evening. The house they stayed in that night, bed and breakfast 2/6d., had a Canadian soldier staying overnight, and over breakfast he told them of his exploits in Norway from where he had just returned. The Germans had just invaded Norway

TELEPHONE : TERMINUS 3300.
TELEGRAMS : "WATER BOARD. SMITH, LONDON."

[M14150]

Metropolitan Water Board.

R. P. MORGAN, F.C.I.S.,
CLERK OF THE BOARD.

ALL LETTERS TO BE ADDRESSED TO
"THE CLERK OF THE BOARD."

IN REPLY PLEASE QUOTE
G.P.128

Clerks Department.
173. Rosebery Avenue, E.C.1.

9th May, 1940.

Dear Sir,

I have the pleasure to inform you that the Board at their meeting today appointed you to the permanent staff in Class II(3) as from 1st February, 1940, at the commencing salary of £90 per annum, subject to your undertaking in writing to join the Superannuation & Provident Fund.

I am,

Yours faithfully,

Clerk of the Board.

Mr. D.A. Moggs,
Comptroller's department.

After over a year on Temporary Staff at 27/6d. per week (£1.37).

fearing a British occupation of that country. Dad said that the intervening years had made him forget what had been said but he remembered how it made them both feel going on a holiday and knowing that even though not much had so far happened in the War, things now seemed to be starting to move and one day something very serious would happen and they too would become directly involved.

Leaving these thoughts behind them, the next day they cycled over Salisbury Plain but once again there were the heavy reminders of war. Convoys of lorries passed, some carrying tanks and guns, others with men yelling and shouting at the two young men on their bicycles – 'They'll get you soon', was the common cry. How true this would be was to be revealed all too soon – Bob was killed in the RAF by enemy action barely two years later.

Dad had never been west of London before and both of the boys relied for their route on a pocket road atlas of Britain which Dad was given at school for getting a distinction in Geography. His father had only ever had one week's holiday a year and, as he was an engine driver on the LNER, all their holiday journeys had been east and north of London, the routes of this railway.

After Salisbury Plain the roads were fairly free of traffic and cycling on near-deserted roads was very pleasant – the weather was kind and Dad said beautiful and, considering it was April, very warm.

Their next stop was Yeovil after visiting Stonehenge which Dad said in those days had no fence and looked as if it was hardly visited – there was no-one in sight for miles around. The following day they went on through Exeter to Torquay and Paignton where they stayed. Dad said the long haul north across Dartmoor was their hardest day. They had gauged the distance they would travel each day from the small map but they had not expected Dartmoor to be so hilly, and they spent a good part of the day walking up hills. At that time Dad said boys didn't have gears on their bicycles, only old men and ladies had three-speed gears – it was considered sissy to have gears. What a difference today when the young are proud to have eighteen or twenty-one gears – men must have been tough half a century ago.

It took some hours to get halfway across the moor and thankfully they at last reached an hotel, Two Bridges, and they were so thirsty and hungry that, in spite of having only two or three pounds to last them the rest of the holiday, they had no alternative but to go in. Dad says he still remembers how awkward he felt sitting in a restaurant in shorts, particularly as he had been used at that time of his life to lesser eating places, and this one he said was quite posh. Fortunately a wartime restriction limited the cost of the meal to five shillings each, but even this was equal to the cost of two nights lodgings with bed and breakfast.

The rest of the holiday Dad says went all too quickly; they visited North Devon, climbing Countisbury Hill and riding hell for leather down Porlock, across Exmoor, the Quantocks, Cheddar Gorge – where Bob fell for a young lady, the daughter of the owner of Goff's Caves, and Dad had a job to get him to cycle on to Bath and then Reading; over 600 miles in the week.

'Truly a holiday to remember in a time when we hardly knew there was a war on,' Dad said. 'I remember it as if it were yesterday – our first holiday from work, sadly it was to be Bob's last. He's buried in Enfield, you know.'

Chapter 4

The Blitz

The holiday over it was back to reality; it was about this time that he said goodbye at work to George and Smithy. George and Smithy were his seniors in the Tottenham Office and had helped him get to know what the work was all about – they were about five years older than him and were off to the forces: George to the Navy – where later he was to become Captain of a minesweeper, whilst Smithy joined the RAF, was later commissioned and became an Observer – later in the war the name Observer was changed to Navigator but by that time poor old Smithy had been killed. Dad believed it was on his first operation shortly after he came to the office resplendent in his officer's uniform. As far as Dad remembers thirty-six aircraft were lost on that raid – Smithy was in a Hampden bomber and a number of planes were lost through severe icing over Norway.

George and Smithy's replacements at the office were two 'old' men who came in as temporaries which was happening all over the country as the young men were called to the colours. One of these men was soon nicknamed 'the judge' after the very popular Hardy films starring Micky Rooney, and became a good friend to Dad, helping him out on fire-watching duties when Dad sometimes turned up late at the office when later he did a door-keeping job. He also taught Dad to use the Morse key – the Judge had been all his life in wireless telegraphy, even being born on Valentia Island off the West coast of Ireland where his father had worked on transatlantic telegraphy for Western Union, or so Dad thought.

Things soon hotted up in the War as Hitler struck into Holland and Belgium in the month after Dad came back from his holiday. Then of course there was Dunkirk and things looked bad – although to the British the retreat from Dunkirk was almost treated as a victory – and of course in

The early fire-watching team at Dad's office in Tottenham Dad, Smithy, George, and Don . . . Summer 1940.

a way it was. France fell and Dad says we were on our own – he always knew the French would give in once Paris had been taken, he said, and had a small bet on it with others in the office who thought otherwise.

Both at home and at the office things went on much the same although a certain tension seemed to grow. On Saturdays Dad went either to the pictures or to a dance – life went on although gradually friends were no longer there or turned up at the dance in uniform. There had still not been any air-raids and all was quiet.

The battle in the air began in the Channel area, slowly at first and then quickening, or so it seemed. The Germans used Stuka bombers attacking convoys and being chased away by Hurricanes and Spitfires. It all still seemed somewhat remote, Dad said, and a radio broadcast of one of these encounters made it all seem even farther away – I have listened to this broadcast as Dad bought the record shortly after and has still got it, and I think I can see what he meant. It was obvious the Stukas were 'easy meat' for our fighters and clearly these dive-bombers had to rely on getting in and out before the fighters were able to be scrambled and arrive on the spot.

Next, as most of us know, following the publicity of the fiftieth anniversary of the Battle of Britain, Dad says the Nazis stepped up their attacks, this time on the airfields in the South, and what later became known as the Battle of Britain had begun. Dad lived in North London and he says the sky to the east of London became covered with vapour trails as the battle raged. Occasionally a German plane would come hurtling down near to home or the office – people would say, 'There's one down in the sewerage farm, two just missed our house and crashed down at the Lock', and so on. Then there would be the thrilling sight of an RAF fighter screaming overhead and rolling over to show he had shot an enemy plane down. It was very exciting and although initially on the sound of the air-raid warning the small staff in the office trooped out to the little shelter behind the office, they spent most of their time outside looking up at what was happening. After a day or so Dad said the shelter was never again used, not even at night in the heavy blitz to come. The daytime battles were very exciting and no-one seemed too concerned that there might be danger out there. The Local Defence Volunteers (LDV) were formed and Grandad having been through the First World War, mostly as a sergeant but being commissioned towards the end, was made an officer and with the rank of First Lieutenant was given charge of the Enfield railway depot LDVs.

Because of the possibility of invasion after Dunkirk all road signs were removed throughout the country and large railway signs were painted out or removed – in fact anything that might help a parachutist know where he was. The blackout was intensified and wardens became more strict in their observance of the rules. Fire-watchers were recruited and streets in London were patrolled at all times of night. At home Dad says it was generally a two hour shift two or three nights a week. On top of this was fire-watching at the office and this meant being away from home sometimes three or four nights each week – on these occasions Dad was excused home fire-watching. Dad was glad of the 'old' men at the office for they took sympathy on him being young and knowing he would soon be in the services, and they co-operated in allowing him off while out with a girl or earning some money as the doorkeeper-cum-bouncer.

Thus life went on whilst the battle in the air was being fought – the importance of it was not fully appreciated at the time. There of course were the daily reports on the wireless and in the papers of how many aircraft were being shot down, and right from the beginning those on the ground knew we were winning and would win – of course in their ignorance Dad said, few of them knew then how stretched the RAF was to

BOROUGH OF EDMONTON. | BDDP | 215 | 4 |

AIR RAID PRECAUTIONS.

𝔗𝔥𝔦𝔰 𝔦𝔰 𝔱𝔬 𝔠𝔢𝔯𝔱𝔦𝔣𝔶 *that* M⅄ . 𝒟 . 𝒜 . 𝘔𝘰𝘨𝘨𝘴.

of 3, Park Ave, *is a member*

of a duly authorised Fire Watchers' Party.

L.P. Parry.
Hon. Organiser.

A.R.P. Controller.

BOROUGH OF EDMONTON
AIR RAID PRECAUTIONS DEPARTMENT

The Fire Precautions (Access to Premises) Order, 1940

THIS IS TO CERTIFY that M.R. D. A. Moggs

of 3 Park Ave. Bush Hill Park. is a member of a fire-fighting party which is recognised by the Edmonton Borough Council and possesses the powers of entry and of taking steps for extinguishing fire or for protecting property, or rescuing persons or property, from fire, which are conferred by the Fire Precautions (Access to Premises) Order, 1940.

JOHN C. SHEFFIELD,

14. 7. 1942.

Controller.

[See over

maintain men in the air or how close they had come to being overwhelmed.

Occasionally, Dad said, he and his friends would decide to go to a cinema up in town – in those days films would play in the West End sometimes weeks before they were put on general release to be seen at local cinemas. The treat of going to the West End cinema could only be occasional as those cinemas charged three or four times as much as the local Savoy or Rialto, etc.

It was on one such visit, when the boys decided to go to the Paramount Tottenham Court Road (strictly not one of the super high-priced West End cinemas) to see Henry Fonda in Steinbeck's *Grapes of Wrath* which had had a big write up in the film weeklies, that it started. Dad thought it was August 24th and must have been a Saturday. As they came out of the cinema in the late afternoon the siren sounded which was soon followed by several explosions, heralding the daylight bombing of London, which Dad reminded me was then by far the largest city in the world. Yes I had previously heard Dad say that London was the largest city and I have checked in encyclopedias of the time and see that it was, not only in population, over nine million (nearly three million more than today), but in area too.

From that day on things happened fast. London became the main target for the Luftwaffe and when the initial day raids over the docks and East End proved too costly in loss of aircraft, the Germans turned to night bombing which continued night after night for many months. Dad said people who did not live through the London Blitz had no conception of what it was like. Of course other towns in Britain were also hit; two, Coventry and Exeter, suffered terribly in single concentrated raids and other large industrial towns had spasmodic raids, but in the Blitz, London had it every night right through to 10 May 1941. It became a way of life; there seemed no end. Life, he said, had to go on and people who lived in London soon accommodated themselves to the disturbance. Thousands were killed, maimed, or made homeless but people went to work, they got married, children were born, grew up, and went to school and took their examinations. Somehow in spite of all the devastation, buses, trams and trains kept running – and Dad says if Grandad were alive today he would laugh at the chaos caused over a few leaves on railway lines – 'They should have been around when we had to keep the railways going – what the bloody hell's a matter with them?' Dad said he would say.

Football and other sports went on but, as in the Phoney War, clubs played not too far away as travel was becoming more difficult, not only was there now bomb damage to deal with but, since all the services had been growing, the railways were becoming overcrowded with troop movements or simply servicemen travelling to and from home on leave. Remember there were few cars and petrol rationing.

At home Dad and his family spent only one or two nights in the Anderson shelter built by Dad and Grandad in the garden during the Munich crisis but it was so uncomfortable that they were quite happy to go back indoors and take their chance. Grandad being an engine driver, whose route at that time was a suburban route to Liverpool Street, of course had often to work at night and was more often than not away from home when the bombing was at its height – he, however, was even more vulnerable driving trains to the very centre of London through all the heavy bombing, watching the City burn and seeing the buildings being devastated at firsthand.

For some time the Germans appeared to be having it their own way; the bombs were falling, searchlights tried to pick them out for the few anti-aircraft guns in use. Then, Dad said, one night – he couldn't remember when it was – everything changed. Observant people must have seen the movement of guns coming in to the very London streets and being set up on waste ground or in parks but these were the few, for Dad said most were completely taken by surprise when suddenly one night, soon after a raid had started, all hell was let loose around with British guns firing. It is really incredible how moral was boosted by this. Next day it was the main topic of conversation both at work and at home – rumours persisted that scores of enemy planes had been shot down; the numbers varied from a dozen to over a hundred. The newspapers added the so-called official score but whatever was correct the value of the gunnery lifted spirits more than anything Dad could recall. In later years it became clear that this was one of Churchill's master strokes. Of course it meant that walking or riding home on a bicycle at night became much more dangerous than previously as shrapnel from our own guns was falling everywhere. Dad says he well remembered many times tearing through North London streets on his bicycle after seeing a girl home wearing a tin hat with shrapnel falling around and wondering whether it was worth staying out so late.

Dad says he and his friends still regularly met at the Spot Club over Burtons in Enfield Town and talk began of whether they wait for the inevitable call-up or volunteer in order to get in the service they wanted. All of the friends who had gone to the Grammar school were to a man going to volunteer for aircrew – all aircrew were volunteers. One or two fellows in their year at school had already gone off and were in. According to the papers Dad's call-up was due for early 1941 – others in the 'gang' born in the year before Dad were due any time. Then it happened; Dad was cycling home from work when suddenly he had bad stomach pains and, getting home, was doubled up and went to bed. A few hours later he collapsed in the toilet and the doctor was called. He was rushed to the North Middlesex Hospital in Edmonton and operated on straightaway at midnight with acute appendicitis.

It was at the height of the Blitz and each night the beds were pulled in to the middle of the wards to keep away from flying glass. In those days persons operated on were confined to bed for several days – in fact although in hospital about two weeks he never once got up – he arrived on a stretcher and went out on a stretcher. It was while in the hospital that the first land mines were dropped on London. These 'bombs' were sent down on parachutes and of course were quite indiscriminate. Two dropped in one night on Tottenham, one considerably less than a mile from the hospital. The devastation was terrific and rows of houses went down like packs of cards although Dad was not to see this for a few weeks. On the same night as the land mines, incendiary bombs hit the hospital and people were rushing hither and thither armed with stirrup pumps and buckets of water. The feeling of helplessness was something Dad remembers but he also remembers the laughs they had amongst the patients watching the antics of the staff. Only minor damage was done to the hospital except to the hospital chapel which was burnt out they were told. Whole streets of houses were destroyed by the land mines in Tottenham and casualties must have been high – goodness knows what the casualties would have been if they had fallen on the hospital.

Whilst away in hospital and work, four of his closest friends, who had been born in the year before Dad and were due to register for call-up, had volunteered for aircrew duties in the RAF. With his friends already in the pipeline for call-up, Dad decided that at his call-up, which was not then far off, he too would volunteer for aircrew.

Back at work one of his older colleagues who ran a small dance band asked him if he would like a job with them as doorkeeper. The wage for doing this included a basic wage plus a share of the takings – the job was to take the money at the door, stop people from getting in without paying (which they considered had cost them a lot in the past) and generally keep the peace. The dances were at halls behind pubs in Barnet and Potters Bar. Dad agreed and for two and three nights a week he carried out this job earning more money in those nights than he earned at the Water Board for working all week.

To get to the dance halls he had to travel by bus – at that time, as all
through the War, the buses were very dimly lit with shades over bulbs and
of course all windows protected by a material stuck to the glass to avoid,
as far as possible, flying glass. The dance halls being on the northern
outskirts of London the bombing was not so bad. In fact Dad says that,
although bombing of London was to some extent indiscriminate, most was
concentrated on the industrial areas, the docks, and of course the City (to
non-Londers the City refers to the old city of London – the square mile in
which relatively few people lived but which was the centre of banking and
commerce) but of course the West End, that is the City of Westminster got
its share too. But the main target were the docks (again at that time the
largest in the world) and industry north and south of the river. In Dad's
area the main targets were the factories along the Lea Valley. Inevitably
residential areas within a mile or two of targets were recipients of a high
proportion of bomb loads whereas some to the west of London at a
distance from concentrated industry or airfields suffered less.

On occasions the bombing forced some of the buses off the road and
Dad would go home with the leader of the band, who was the drummer
and vocalist, and who drove a motorbike and sidecar. Dad was squashed
in the sidecar holding a drum all the way to Muswell Hill whilst watching
the searchlights and gun flashes overhead – he could hear nothing only the
roar of the motorbike as they tore along the streets Dad hanging on to the
drum round corners as the driver who must, as Dad said, have thought he
was Stanley Woods. Stanley Woods, Dad told me, was the Isle of Man TT
rider who pre-war won many of the races on his 500cc Norton.

Dad says he enjoyed the job and met many interesting people – much of
the evening it was fairly quiet but as soon as the bars closed it was then
that he had sometimes to use his muscle, as in the mad rush there were
many who 'forgot' to pay. However, Dad was no weakling and was
prepared to mix it should there be trouble – very seldom was there trouble
as men seemed to sense that Dad was no 'easy meat'. He of course did his
job enthusiastically not least because he was on a share of the gate.

The dance halls and surrounding area being on the outskirts of London
missed major damage but one was always aware of what was going on
outside and there was always the stray or lost bomber who dropped his
load anywhere before going home.

Near Christmas 1940 Dad was invited to an all-night party – the first he
had ever been to – in Edmonton, managing to get there, really in no fit
state, after drinking in a local pub with the boys. It was at this party that
Dad met Betty, and it is from their correspondence through the years that

follow which has been of the utmost help in providing additional background to this story. The letters are a story in themselves and I could not hope to summarize the contents of so many letters – there are over 1,100 most of which consist of about 700 words each with many of very much greater length, with possibly close to a million words in total, enough for several average books.

Betty worked as a telephonist for an insurance company who had earlier that year left the City and taken over a country mansion in Bedfordshire, a place called Wrest Park in the village of Silsoe. She came home some weekends but otherwise stayed in the country.

Of the correspondence in 1941 and much of 1942 between Dad and Betty, only those letters written by him were kept but after this time all letters written by both parties have been carefully retained. I will from time to time include extracts, or even photocopies of whole letters, which I consider may help the younger reader understand what it was like to be a young person in the war years so long ago. However, in all truth, the letters are mostly telling how these two young people, so obviously in love, spent their time whilst apart.

Early on Dad writes:

> 'Bush Hill Park, Enfield, 6th May 1941 . . . How about coming for a ride Saturday afternoon if it's fine – I'll be down by the cemetery about 2.30 pm, I'll wait 10 minutes and if you don't come by then I'll know you have already arranged to go out – or you haven't cleaned your bicycle or that you don't want to go for a ride or that seeing me once in a day is enough. But seriously if the weather is fine – I mean sun shining – I'd like to go for a ride, or I might even come along and clean your bicycle – maybe!
>
> I've just thought of the third to tell you – I am playing football Wednesday evening on Enfield's ground, Ron is going to do my job at Barnet – wish me luck (its too late, it'll be all over by the time you get this). Hope you enjoy or should I say enjoyed the dance at Henlow – I'm terribly jealous, . . .'

Sometimes very little mention is made of the War but in other letters the whole atmosphere of the time is brought to life; the job is to find time to read all the letters and decide what should best be shown. Quite early on in their relationship Dad said he was able on one or two occasions to go up to Bedfordshire on a Sunday to see Betty but otherwise from the time he first met her until well after the War had ended he generally only met her at a weekend or when on leave from work or the services. The journey to Silsoe was by train from St Pancras to Luton and then a ten-mile ride by bus. Dad said it was another world up there, for apart from RAF stations in the area there was absolutely no sign of a war. Things changed somewhat later when the Americans eventually entered the War and took over stations in the area. The George Hotel, Pear Tree Cottage and another local pub were favourite haunts for the 'evacuees' and their guests.

However, I am in danger of jumping ahead. The Blitz was still raging and casualties were mounting. Of the stories he told me I remember one which obviously touched Dad a good deal. He said there had been a particular bad night of bombing with some obviously falling quite near to his home. Late that night there was a knock at the door and when Dad opened the door, always with the light out because of the blackout, he was asked by a tearful man if his Dad was there. It turned out to be Grandad's fireman who had come to the door. It seems his house in the next street had been bombed and he had lost everything; luckily he and his wife had been in the shelter when the house had been hit. Dad said the man crying would always stay in his mind.

Another incident was when early in the new year (1941) he had been due to go to Prince's Hall in Wood Green, in North London. Although he had the doorkeeping job they did not often require him on Saturdays as they already employed two men on what was usually a busier night. Dad mostly being free on a Saturday had been going regularly to this hall on both Saturdays and Sundays (he had joined the Sunday club) – he often went on his own. Dad was a good dancer, so everyone told him, he said, and he did in fact enter a competition once with a young lady who after the War won with her husband the first Victor Sylvester television dancing competition. Be this as it may, on the night in question he had quite suddenly decided to go to a dance nearer his home as he had learnt that the young lady he had met at the all-night party, Betty, was going there too. He was certainly pleased he did change his mind for not only did he begin a very happy and long-lasting relationship with the young lady but missed being involved in a tragedy as the Prince's Hall was bombed and twenty-eight people were killed in the hall and on a trolley bus passing at the time. When there was a particularly nasty incident such as this the news soon spread and Dad's friend, Ron, for whom shortly Dad would become his best man, came post-haste to his home to find out if Dad was OK as he was certain Dad would have been at the hall. Why did not he telephone, I hear you say. Well practically no-one had telephones in their homes at that time; the telephone in nearly every home came some years after the war.

E.D.M.

FORM C 2
Form Issued by the
(Individual Certificate)

MINISTRY OF HOME SECURITY and the SCOTTISH HOME DEPARTMENT

CERTIFICATE relating to the number of hours of Fire Prevention Duties which a person is deemed to have undertaken, or to be required, to perform outside his working hours in a prescribed 4-weekly period at business premises to which the Fire Prevention (Business Premises) (No. 2) Order, 1941, applies.

Issued for the purposes of Paragraph (7) incorporated in Article 4 of the Civil Defence Duties (Compulsory Enrolment) Order, 1941, by Article 1 of the Civil Defence Duties (Compulsory Enrolment) (No. 3) Order, 1941.

If the holder of this Certificate has been registered under the Civil Defence Duties (Compulsory Enrolment) Order 1941 in the area where he resides and desires to claim exemption (either total or partial) from enrolment by the local authority for performance of fire prevention duties in that area or if, having already been enrolled, he desires to be released by the local authority from performance of all or part of those duties, he should send or take the Certificate to the person authorised by the local authority for completion of Part 2 of the Certificate.

PART 1 (to be completed by the occupier or other authorised person)
1. Name in full of holder of Certificate...... HOGGS, DONALD ALLEN
(Surname first, in BLOCK CAPITALS)
2. Date of birth..... 23.1.1922
3. National Registration Identity No. BDDP 215/4
4. Private address 3, Park Avenue, Bush Hill Park, Enfield Mddx
5. Name of occupier of business premises ...... METROPOLITAN WATER BOARD.
6. Address(es) of business premises at which fire prevention duties are performed...... 551 B. High Rd Bruce Grove. Tottenham. N.17.
7. Date of expiry of Certificate...... 31 MAY 1942

8. Certificate.—I hereby certify that the above-named person has undertaken, or is required to perform outside his working hours at the above-named business premises fire prevention duties under arrangements in force for these premises under the Fire Prevention (Business Premises) (No. 2) Order, 1941, and that the number of hours, duly calculated in accordance with the provisions of paragraph (7B) incorporated in Article 4 of the Civil Defence Duties (Compulsory Enrolment) Order, 1941, by Article 1 of the Civil Defence Duties (Compulsory Enrolment) (No. 3) Order, 1941, is :—

Date of Signature of Certificate...... 10 FEB 1942   ...... One H..... hours. (See Notes 3 and 4.)
Signature...... E. A. Brown
(To be signed only (a) by the occupier of the business premises, or (b) by a person with the approval of the appropriate authority, or (c) by a person of a class so authorised.)

Note 1.—Where in any prescribed period of 12 weeks a Certificate is issued to a person during the first 4 weeks of that period, the Certificate will expire at the end of that 12-weekly period : but, where such a Certificate is issued during the last 8 weeks of a 12-weekly period, the Certificate will remain valid until the expiry of the next succeeding 12-weekly period, provided that the holder continues to perform fire prevention duties under the arrangements in force for the premises.

Note 2.—The validity of this Certificate may be extended by endorsement in the spaces provided overleaf not more than three times. A Certificate should, as far as practicable, be so endorsed not less than four weeks and not more than eight weeks before the date of expiry of the Certificate or of the current endorsement as

the case may be. When a Certificate is so endorsed, the occupier or other authorised person must enter in the space provided in the endorsement the number of hours which, for the period covered by the endorsement, the holder of the Certificate is deemed to have undertaken, or to be required, to perform at the premises outside his working hours whether or not that number is the same as that entered against Item 8 of the original Certificate.

Note 3.—Where the number to be entered against Item 8 exceeds 30, it will be sufficient to enter " over 30 ".

Note 4.—During the period covered by an endorsement of this Certificate the figure shown against Item 1 of that endorsement is deemed to be substituted for the figure shown against Item 8 of this Certificate.

PART 2 (to be completed, in accordance with the table given below, by the local authority of the area in which the holder resides.)
The number of hours of fire prevention duties for which the holder of the Certificate is liable to be called upon by the local authority in any prescribed 4-weekly weeks covered by the Certificate is...... NIL ......hours.
Date...... 17 MAR 1942   Signature......
(being a person duly authorised by the Council of EDMONTON.

Table showing the number of hours (if any) of fire prevention duties for which the holder of this Certificate is liable to be enrolled, in a prescribed 4-weekly period, by the local authority in whose area he resides, unless he is otherwise exempt.

Number of hours of fire prevention duties shown against Item 8 above or in the relevant endorsement hereunder.	Number of hours of fire prevention duties for which the holder may be enrolled by the local authority.
Nil (no Certificate is required in this case)	48
Not more than 6	36
More than 6 but not more than 18	24
More than 18 but not more than 30	12
Over 30	Nil

[P.T.O.

Another story Dad mentioned, but didn't say too much about, was the awful job he had to call on homes in blitzed areas. After the main bombing, later called the Blitz, ceased in May 1941, and May 10th was a particularly bad night, Dad was sent by his employers to check on which houses were being lived in, so there was a record of at least who should be paying water rates. It seems strange that there would be people worrying about water rates whilst all hell was being let loose around. But as Dad said life had to go on, water was essential, and people had to be employed and they had to be paid in order to carry on living, and the money had to be collected to pay them. Dad had an area in central and south Tottenham which he had taken over from George and Smithy when they went into the services, and some of the devastation in those areas was too terrible to describe. Hardly any houses that stood had glass in the windows and most looked empty but he was soon to discover that most of those still standing were indeed occupied and some of the people who came to the door Dad could hardly look at – many were disfigured beyond belief – and he said it made him feel quite ill. Fire-watching was carried on all through the Blitz and after. As far as I remember Dad said all streets were organised into fire-watching groups in connection with the local wardens employed by the council – the latter were mostly full-time. A rota was prepared so that pairs could patrol their street during the night – women and men were involved. There was also compulsory fire-watching on commercial premises which generally took precedence over local watching. Dad was required to fire-watch on a rota basis on the offices in which he worked in Tottenham but since they were a small staff at the office it meant being there several nights a week. He shared the watch with mostly 'old' men who had joined the Water Board to fill gaps left by the young leaving for the services. There was the Judge, mentioned above, Mac, Ted and the under-boss, Charlie – all good sorts who turned a blind eye to Dad arriving late, sometimes in the middle of the night when he had been on the door of one of the dances or been out with a young lady. Sleep was not easy and although bombing was going on much of the time it could be a bit of a bind being there and having little to do.

The Blitz ended suddenly, although of course Londoners were unaware that it had ended; the last heavy raid of the blitz was 10 May 1941 which was the time Germany invaded Russia. London was to get hundreds of raids over the next years but none were to be so sustained as the Blitz until Germany introduced the Flying Bomb and the V-2 rockets in 1944-45.

Chapter 5

The Long Wait

I asked Dad what his general recollections of how life was at this time in the War, what were people thinking and how did they think the War would end. Strangely, he said, he never once heard anybody bother about saying how they thought the War would end – everyone knew we would win eventually, and this was before the Americans entered the War. Moral was kept high by speeches on the wireless by Churchill, and of course the reports of our planes bombing Germany every night. We also knew the Royal Navy ruled the seas, for had we not made the Germans scuttle the *Graf Spee* in the Battle of the River Plate. Convoys were getting through protected by the Navy – the U-boat menace was serious, but the Germans had yet to show if they could match the Royal Navy on the water. In May after losing HMS *Hood* the *Bismarck* was sunk and Germany had only one major battleship left – the *Tirpitz*. Then the Army had some victories in North Africa when General Wavell with 30,000 men captured some 200,000 Italians. When in June Germany invaded Russia it became even more certain that they would lose the War and even when they were close in on Moscow and Leningrad, Dad said, the sureness of the eventual victory for Britain and the Empire was never in doubt in the minds of the average man in the street.

During this period Dad continued with his work at the office during the day whilst many nights were spent fire-watching at home or at the office. In the evenings he carried on with his work at the dances or went out with his friends or with a girl – or even stayed home!

He continued playing football, his first love, whenever he got the chance and remembers turning out for Grandad's Home Guard in a match against another unit which was played on Enfield's Football Ground.

It was about this time that my Auntie Babs, Dad's sister, married a sergeant in the Army who Dad remembers as a footballer and who had been on the books of Derby County.

Three of his close friends who had volunteered for aircrew duties in the RAF, while Dad was in hospital, were due away in the New Year.

Dad registered and volunteered himself for aircrew early in 1941. However, from then on everything seemed to conspire to keep him from going into the services.

There were two medicals which had to be passed before being accepted for aircrew training. The first was the general medical for acceptance in the RAF which in Dad's case took place at Kings Cross early in 1941 whilst the Blitz was at its height. He did not pass the medical but was referred back for further examination of his heart since he had had rheumatic fever as a child. He was to be given an appointment with a Harley Street specialist. This is an example, Dad said, as to how relaxed everyone was in spite of Britain being up against what was then the most powerful nation in the world. The RAF needed aircrew but nevertheless they were making sure that only those 100 per cent fit would get in.

The appointment with the Harley Street specialist came several weeks later. He said he remembers the doctor made him climb up and down off a stool and then he had to put his foot into a vessel full of water wired up to something, but what it was he has forgotten.

He is sure he could have got out of going into the services at all for the doctor gave him the option: 'Do you really want to go into the services young man; you have good reason not to, you know.' Dad of course did not take up the offer – how could he, he said, when not only was it his duty but so many of his school friends were already in.

The medical was therefore passed and Dad had to wait to be called again for what was known as the aircrew medical.

Weeks became months and life went on, working in the day at the office, acting as doorkeeper/bouncer generally three evenings a week, going to the cinema or a dance, acting as home contact for friends in the services and accompanying them on a night out when on a spot of leave, and seeing his girlfriend, Betty, on those weekends she was able to come home or occasionally Dad going up to Silsoe for a day. Then there was all the letter writing not only to Betty but as I see from his letters to her keeping up correspondence particularly with three of his friends who went into the RAF in '41 – Bob, Del and Ron. The latter married Bob's sister in the summer of 1941 and Dad was Ron's best man.

'Bush Hill Park, Enfield, 20th October 1941 . . . To make things worse I heard a rotten piece of news this morning while going up in the train, a fellow who was in my form at school and who had recently become a pilot in the RAF, has just been reported missing . . .'

'Bush Hill Park, Enfield, 3rd November 1941 . . . The wireless is on and I can't concentrate very well . . . Today has been very cold and I have been a little depressed . . . I had to go out on the 'district' and took the opportunity to visit a shop in Wood Green and put a deposit on a watch for you – so please make certain nobody else is going to get you one. I would like you to come shopping with me next Saturday week so that I can buy a few Xmas presents. We could go up the West End or somewhere . . . I'm afraid the supply of chocolates this week-end will not be good – I tried at lunch-time but was unsuccessful, the shortage seems to be getting more serious . . .

Tomorrow I have got to do fire-watching at the office, Wednesday I'm at the Lion, Thursday I am going out with Ron and Friday the usual happens – I will be staying at Varnier's on Friday night. How about coming to watch me play football – as I told you I am playing for the Masters against the 1st XI of the School – should be quite a good match . . .

I've been telling everybody at work about "the 49th parallel" – a marvellous film wasn't it . . .'

Although the intensive nightly bombing of London has ceased on May 10th there were of course many other raids to keep the population wondering when Jerry would strike again. The latter's main effort had been transferred to the Eastern Front and for some time the Germans had been pressing at the gates of Moscow and Leningrad. Elsewhere in the world Dad seems to remember there might have been some news of verbal unfriendliness between the USA and Japan but no-one took much notice of it.

During '41 Dad had to attend the National Dental Hospital in Great Portland Street where his under-boss's son, Gordon, was a student. Dad it seems had a bad abscess which a surgeon eventually had to remove by operation (an apus sectomy Dad says he thinks it was called), he also had to have a number of teeth filled by Gordon who, as with all the students, took many visits to finish. This was before the National Health Scheme and dental treatment had to be paid for but, being a training hospital if you

Barnet Football Club.

President.
N B ASHWORTH, Esq.

Chairman.
G. SANDERSON, Esq.

Hon. Treasurer.
A. E. WHITTAKER.

MEMBERS OF
THE FOOTBALL ASSOCIATION   THE ATHENIAN LEAGUE
AFFILIATED TO HERTS AND LONDON F.A.'S

COLOURS-AMBER AND BLACK JERSEYS, WHITE KNICKERS.

HEADQUARTERS-"QUEENS ARMS." BARNET   PHONE-BARNET 0156
GROUND-UNDERHILL STADIUM BARNET   PHONE-BARNET 2052

Hon. Secretary.
L J. PURROTT.
Phone BARNET 0346

Press Sec. and
Hon. Assistant Sec.
H. SWIFT.
Phone-BARNET 4367

3, Strafford Villas,
Hadley,
BARNET.

24th November, 1941.

D.A.Moggs, Esq.,
551B, High Road,
TOTTENHAM, N.17.

Dear Mr.Moggs,

I understand from Mr.Lester Finch that you would like a game with
our reserve side on Saturday next, and wish to confirm the arrangements made
for you to be at our ground at Underhill, Barnet, in good time for the
kick-off which, I believe, is timed for 3.15 p.m.   The time of the kick-off
may be altered to 3 p.m. so please do not be late.

Mr.G.R.Middleton, the Vice-Chairman of the Club, will be at the
ground, and if you will enquire for him he will introduce you to the Team
Secretary, Mr.Dennis Young.

Best wishes for a good and successful game.

Yours faithfully,

Hon.Secretary.

didn't mind the students working on you, one could get it carried out for sixpence a visit! No injections for fillings in those days.

Whilst attending this hospital Dad met a student who he had on more than one occasion played football against (an ex-pupil of Minchenden School) and Dad was asked whether he would help the hospital, then associated with Charing Cross Hospital, in a couple of games as they were short. Thus it came about that Dad turned out and played for Charing Cross Hospital. And later with Gordon, who also played for the hospital, he was invited to play with Barnet F.C. through the good offices of Lester Finch, then an international playing with professional teams as a guest player.

However, Dad soon got fed up playing football on Saturdays as it was generally the only time he could see Betty and sometimes he would not get back until late Saturday night. For example, to get to Barnet's ground at Underhill he had to get a train to Enfield Town and then take a bus ride of about thirty minutes to Barnet. Coaches were generally laid on for away matches but Dad still had to travel back on the bus and train to his home.

He was sorry to give up football but he knew he would soon be in the forces and in any case he says he often played at a higher standard when in the RAF, playing in many teams with professionals on both sides.

'Bush Hill Park, Enfield, 3rd Dec 1941 . . . Oh, I had a card from Barnet F.C. today saying I'm to meet the team at the Queen's Arms next to the Odeon (Barnet) at 1.30 on Saturday. A coach is taking us from there . . . if we wish to bring a friend along we can and the cost is 2/6. It's a pity you've got Pam coming otherwise I could have taken you – it would have been a nice coach ride even if you didn't like the game . . .'

'Bush Hill Park, Enfield, 16th December 41 . . . My father went to hospital today they told him he had a rupture but that they will not operate until after the war as he is in work of National importance – I expect they'll give him a truss. I do hope they don't make him wait too long for it because it gives him terrific pain sometimes.'

About this time Dad at last got his call for his second medical. He could not remember a great deal of what happened when there, except he remembers well the eyes, ears, nose and throat doctor who pushed one finger to the side of Dad's nostrils and told him to breath. Dad was OK on one side but not on the other; he was completely blocked and failed the medical. He was told that the only way to get into aircrew would be to have an operation to remove the offending bone which the doctor said must have been caused by a heavy blow on the nose. He would have to go to his own doctor and arrange the operation himself and when done the hospital would inform the RAF.

'Bush Hill Park, Enfield, 20th January 1942 . . . Well I haven't long been back from Euston and what a time I had. I was there from 8.30 am to 5.00 pm. I passed the writing tests (you know Maths, General Knowledge etc.) and then went to the 'selection board' – they passed me for pilot. Then started the real ordeal – the medical. It's in and out of different rooms all the time – then they wouldn't pass me completely. Oh yes I shall pass eventually, I hope, but first I have to have an operation on my nose. You remember I told you I couldn't breath through my right nostril – or maybe I never told you – well they discovered this and told me I have to go to hospital and have it put right . . .'

On arriving home his mother said he was mad to contemplate having an operation in order to get into aircrew. However, Dad was determined: he did not want to be different from his friends.

'Bush Hill Park, Enfield, 27th January 1942 . . . I went to the hospital this morning and after a very long wait managed to see the specialist – he examined me and pulled my nose about a bit and told me the hospital would let me know when I must go. I expect it will be pretty soon . . .

Dad's letter goes on to say he went to work in the afternoon and then off to the cinema where he saw two good films one of which was Sonja Henie and John Payne in *Sun Valley Serenade* which featured the Glenn Miller orchestra. I smiled when I saw Dad's efforts at describing a new tune he liked, 'The Chatanooga Choo Choo'.

'I can't remember the correct title but its something like 'The —— —— choo choo chootaga!' – probably nothing like it but it's all about a train.'

After describing his proposed activities for the week he then goes on to ask,

'What do you think of the first day of the big debate in the House
of Commons? It doesn't look too good does it. Churchill seems to
think the war will last at least another two years.'

Although the Americans were forced into the War in December '41 none
of Dad's letters refer to this, which seems to reinforce the notion that the
British people then did not think the Americans would make that much
difference as they were going to win anyway.

Arrangements were made through his local doctor for a visit to the
Prince of Wales hospital in Tottenham and bearing in mind the shortage of
beds due to war casualties it was not surprising that he had to wait.
Eventually he was found a bed in a hospital in Wanstead. Some months
had passed since the medical, the Blitz had ended and his friends who had
joined earlier in the year were already abroad in Canada and America
training for aircrew.

I asked Dad what he thought had caused him to have a blocked nose and
he smiled. He said he knew very well what had caused it and related the
following. Dad and some friends were leaving a fair ground just before the
War when, because of bumping into someone in the half-light, words were
exchanged which ended in a fight. Dad who had done a lot of boxing at
school and who had a father who was proud of the fact that he had had the
gloves on with Bombadier Billy Wells when the latter was Heavy Weight
Champion of Britain, had come up against a real tough nut who was obviously used to street fighting. Dad was badly beaten and it transpired later
that the man was from the Boxing Booth, the recognised training ground
for professionals. It was hardly boxing, however, when his opponent got
Dad's head under his arm and pummelled his nose – Dad was only sixteen.

He remembered the operation on his nose quite vividly as it was carried
out under a local anaesthetic. His face was covered except for his nose and
the surgeon seemed to hammer the blockage clear with an instrument that
must have been a small sledge hammer. After the operation and back in
the ward the Sister who had attended the operation said, 'Did that hurt
you, Ginger?' Dad told her he was in considerable pain all the time with
the hammering. 'Why didn't you say so – I had a bet with the surgeon that
you were suffering as I could see your feet moving.' Yes, Dad said, his
mum had been right when she told him he was mad to have the operation.
He was in hospital a week and when he came out he had to notify the RAF
that he was now ready to be checked again. Several more weeks later he
was called again and this time passed the medical. However, by this time
the number of aircrew in training or to be trained was so great that there

NATIONAL SERVICE (ARMED FORCES) ACTS

MINISTRY OF LABOUR
MINISTRY OF LABOUR AND NATIONAL SERVICE
EMPLOYMENT

NATIONAL

Local Office,........................

TEL. No. TOTT, 5074.

TOTTENHAM, N.17.

2 6 AUG '4?

Registration No. £ .N7.22574. ....(Date)

MR..... D. A. Moggs.
3. Park Avenue
Bush Hill Park
Enfield

DEAR SIR,

I have to inform you that in accordance with the National Service (Armed Forces) Acts you are required to submit yourself to medical examination by a medical board at .... a.m. on .... Tues,day, ... SEP '4? .....19.. at the Medical p.m. Board Centre, Drill Hall. Dukes Rd. Euston.

If you wear glasses, you should bring them with you to the Medical Board.

On reporting for medical examination you should present this form and your Certificate of Registration (N.S. 2) to the clerk in charge of the waiting room.

*A Travelling Warrant for your return journey is enclosed. Before starting your journey you must exchange the warrant for a ticket at the booking office named on the warrant. You should take special care of the return half of the ticket as in the event of loss you will be required to obtain a fresh ticket at normal fare at your own expense.

*If you reside more than six miles from the Medical Board Centre and travel by omnibus or tram your fare will be paid at the Centre.

Any expenses or allowances which may become payable to you in accordance with the scale overleaf will be paid to you on application when you attend at the Medical Board Centre.

Immediately on receipt of this notice, you should inform your employer of the date and time at which you are required to attend for medical examination.

If you are called up you will receive a further notification giving you at least three days' notice. You should accordingly not voluntarily give up your employment because you are required to attend for medical examination.

Your attention is directed to the Notes printed on the back of this Notice.

Yours faithfully,

N.S.6

* Delete if not applicable

COLIN FORSYTH
Manager. P.T.O.

B

(To be torn off and given to recipient, who should retain it in order to prove his identity)

Royal Air Force Volunteer Reserve Badge.

I, (No. **1804757** MOGGS. D. A. ....

hereby acknowledge receipt of Royal Air Force Volunteer Reserve Badge No. ...78981.... I clearly understand that this badge remains the property of the Air Ministry and that I am liable to surrender it on being called upon to do so by my superior officer.

....
(Signature of recipient.)

(Sgd.) C. B. McWeeney.
....
(Signature of Officer Commanding Recruits Centre.)

~~Recruits Centre.~~)

.......................(No.
10 APR 1942
.......................(Date.)

Wt. 22474/4302 20M 7/41 H. & C./9647 G745

was a waiting period. Recruits were given their service number and sent home on deferred leave – it was estimated it would be five months but turned out to be eight months before he was eventually called.

These men were given a tiny silver badge to put in their lapel to make people aware they were in the RAF. The badge was pretty useless as Dad well remembers when on one occasion whilst at work a Jewish barber in West Green Road, Tottenham, from whom Dad was trying to collect his water-rate, told him he ought to be in the services. Dad says he pointed to his badge informing the man he was already in and told him that unless he apologised he would come round to see him after work – the man apologised and paid his overdue water-rate without a murmur. Yes, Dad said, it made him think and wondered how many other people really knew what the tiny badge with the letters RAFVR (Royal Air Force Volunteer Reserve) really meant.

Then came the biggest blow of the lot – his friend Bob with whom he had shared the cycling holiday was reported killed. Dad says he remembers the circumstances well but not the date – one evening on the radio the announcer going through the news of the day reported that the fighter ace, Paddy Finucane, had been reported missing over the sea and that one of our air-sea rescue launches in the search, had been fired upon by a German plane and that one member of the crew had been killed – the mention of this incident showed the Germans in the worst possible light as the announcer went on to say that these rescue launches picked up German crewmen as well as the allied airmen. It was later that evening that Dad learnt that the airman killed was his friend Bob.

Bob was brought to Enfield to be buried and given a full military funeral by the RAF with his friends in uniform acting as bearers – unfortunately Dad was not asked to be a bearer as he had no uniform. He knows the RAF would not have minded but Bob's father only wanted uniformed men. Dad says it hurt a lot as he had done everything to get into the services and he was one of Bob's best friends.

It must have been devastating for the parents particularly as earlier that year Bob's older brother, Doug, an Army Officer, had been in Singapore when it fell to the Japs. Whether his parents knew he was a prisoner at that time Dad could not remember. However, he told me Doug did survive the privations of a Japanese POW camp and on return to civilian life reached the very top of his profession with a seat on the main board of Barclays Bank – General Manager, I think.

It was at this point that Dad left the War to tell me a little post-war anecdote concerning Doug. It was some forty or so years after the War when quite by chance when listening to the radio he discovered Doug had reached such exalted heights and, as his company at that time was having some money problems in Nigeria, thought he would see if his old friend's brother could offer any help. After all, Dad said, the three of them had before the War paid six shillings each to buy a new football (a T-ball for 90p!) and since the ball had been kept at the brother's house and Dad had not seen it since the War, he reckoned Doug owed him one – six shillings in fact, and told his secretary so. It must have worked and although Doug never talked to Dad he did bring power to bear on others in the bank – in fact the boss of Barclays Overseas did all he could to help although Dad's company banked elsewhere.

'I reckon we're even now!' Dad said.

His thoughts back to the funeral he was reminded of others in the 'gang' who he thinks must have acted as bearers – Eric became a fighter pilot and was shot down over Jugoslavia and badly injured, Del became a bomber pilot and was in his third tour with a Pathfinder squadron when shot down over Germany and taken prisoner, Bill was also a bomber pilot and after being shot down – presumably over France, was guided by the French Resistance over the Alps and down to Gibraltar, and Ron who was also in the RAF and ended the War, Dad thinks, in the Middle East.

Most of those mentioned were from Dad's last school, Enfield Grammar, and of course there were others from that school who would be injured or killed before the War came to an end. He has never been back to the school since the War to see any memorial, unlike the visit he said he made in 1990 to his other old school in Romford, the Royal Liberty, the first visit there he told me since he had left in 1937 – he sadly found many old class mates listed on the memorial in the hall.

However, at the time of Bob's death this was the first close friend to be killed. Of course there was poor old Smithy at the office who was killed on what Dad believed was his first raid over Germany.

Again Dad seemed to be confused on dates before going in the services and he mentioned to me a number of incidents that occurred in the waiting period. One I think worth reporting was when his friend Del, a school friend with whom Dad had spent a lot of time pre-war and the early part of the War playing snooker, table tennis, dancing, drinking, etc., got himself injured whilst in the RAF training as a pilot. Del had kept up correspondence with both Dad and his friend Ron, the latter on ground staff in the RAF stationed at that time in London. Ron and my Dad decided to try and visit Del in hospital in Ely one Sunday when Ron had leave from camp. It of course had to be by train and, since the main line to

Cambridge went through a part of Enfield, they managed to catch a slow train to Ely.

Ron was in uniform and having duly found the hospital, which was RAF and then Del, they went to have something to eat; Del having smashed his kneecap was now recovering and was walking wounded. However, going to eat on the camp posed a problem as Dad was a civilian so Del, who had recently spent twenty-eight days in the glasshouse for low flying over Peterborough, said that if asked Dad should say he was on leave from Cardington – no-one was going to ask said Del reassuringly. Just Dad's luck for the station padre buttoned on to Dad and asked him where he was from – Dad duly said Cardington, whereupon the padre said he knew it well and proceeded to ask some awkward questions which Dad managed to counter but for a while it became most embarrassing.

Dad remembers Ely hospital well but was very glad to get out of the Airmen's Mess.

Looking at some of the scores of letters written between Dad and his wife-to-be Betty, I found one about this period which was worth a mention. It seems that the Government set up Communal Restaurants throughout the country and Dad sometimes went along to one of these set up in a school in Tottenham.

The menu is worth repeating: Stewed Steak, Haricot Beans, Boiled Potatoes and Gravy – Bread Pudding and a cup of Tea. Price 9*d*!

Mind you when Dad could afford a midday meal at work he generally preferred the little Italian café where he could get Roast Beef, Yorkshire Pudding and two Veg for eleven pence ha'penny, that's less than 5p today – of course he only earned about £1.50 a week.

Of course, Dad reminded at one session, America had come in the War in this time. No-one who has television needs reminding what happened to bring them into it – Pearl Harbour, 7 December 1941. How many films about it or which refer to it I am sure no-one knows, but the reaction of ordinary people in the UK, Dad remembered, was quite different from what one might have expected when looking back at the part eventually played by the Americans in the War. Strangely people did not look upon this change in events as being of any great help to us. We would win on our own anyway being the general feeling – Dad says he never remembers anyone who ever thought we would lose the War, it was just a matter of time. Why this was can only be attributed to school upbringing and pride – he said they had been taught at school that the British Empire was the biggest the world had ever known; how could anyone think they could beat us and how did anyone think they could win by bombing London –

how could they possibly flatten London which then was by far the biggest city in the world with a population of over nine million (over two million more than it is today), twice the size of Berlin and bigger than New York.

Yes, Dad said, it was a matter of time, but there was no illusion over how long it would take before it ended – it became a way of life. It was now heading for eighteen months since he had first volunteered for aircrew and it seemed he would never get in.

He became engaged to my brother's mother, Betty, and, although not formally seeking permission of her father, wondered whether he should have done, as her dad was then in his sixties and seemed to be from a bygone age – a typical Edwardian and one of the nicest men Dad said he had ever met. Sadly he died not long afterwards. The engagement ring of a small emerald and two big diamonds cost £11.00 and was bought in South Tottenham.

In talking and listening to Dad it was obvious that just talking and thinking back made him suddenly remember things he had forgotten to tell me. It was in one of these sessions that he suddenly remembered that he had joined the ATC (Air Training Corps) – it seems that he joined with another friend who had also volunteered for aircrew and they went along together to his old school (Enfield Grammar school) where a unit of the Corps had been established. Most of those in the Corps were younger than Dad and his friend who had simply joined to cover the period between getting a number in the RAF and awaiting the official call to arms – there was no intention of them having uniforms but simply to attend lectures. These covered Navigation, Meterology, Mathematics, and Morse Code plus general matters on the RAF such as learning the various ranks and how these compared with those in the Army and Navy. Dad still has two books from the ATC – both are in pristine condition as if just purchased and looked unused. Perhaps Dad thought he knew it all! The books are *Mathematics for the ATC* price 1/9 and *Practical Navigation for the A.T.C.* not priced. He cannot remember much about going to ATC but thinks they attended only once a week – he says he could not imagine it was more often as he had a very busy life then what with acting as a doorkeeper two and three nights a week, fire-watching at both the office and at home and, in the winter, playing football, and then of course there was dancing and of course his fiancée, Betty.

He told me how when Betty was on weekend duty, she was a telephonist and had to take a turn on the switchboard for part of some weekends, he would try to get to see her. He had to get up to London (people who live in the suburbs always talk about going up to London, or they did in his day), take a train from St Pancras to Luton, and then a bus for ten miles to the village of Silsoe. Her company, The Sun Fire Insurance Company, had been evacuated from Threadneedle St. in the City at the beginning of the War.

Betty helped run a group of Brownies in the village, a Brown Owl, Dad thinks, and later joined the Home Guard. Dad said he never heard of other women in the Home Guard but he guesses there must have been a few in other parts of the country – anyway it was something the writer of *Dad's Army* seems to have missed.

Chapter 6

The Call to Arms

Finally it happened – he received his calling-up papers. He was told to report to Aircrew Reception Centre – known within the services as ACRC – in London. The reception centre itself was in fact Lord's Cricket ground. He had only been to Lord's once before and that was when he was at school in Essex – there had been a school outing to see one of their old boys play for England against the West Indies. The boy was Kenneth Farnes, the Essex and England fast bowler, who was sadly killed in the War whilst in the RAF. Dad hesitated in his story as he tried to recall some details from the visit which must have been in the mid-thirties but his mind was blank; he only knew he was there.

Back to the story, Dad said his mind was equally blank when he tried to remember leaving home to join the RAF or going to Lord's, or how his civilian clothes eventually got back to his home – perhaps he said they never did. Anyway, he was obviously issued with a uniform and all the other clothes that formed a part of that necessary to become an airman with the rank of AC2 (the lowest form of animal life in the RAF). He was then sent to one of the nearby blocks of flats then requisitioned by the RAF. He was first of all in 6, Hall Road and later he seems to remember he was moved to Grove Road. In all he was there nine weeks and it was there that he got his first taste of square-bashing and made to realise how low an AC2 was considered. Most of the lads were younger than him and were, with few exceptions, either Grammar School or Public School boys. The standard required for a pilot or navigator was quite tough and it was said that aircrew took the cream of the young men if they could get them. Dad was close to twenty-one and most of the others were just eighteen and at that age three years made a big difference.

Dad says he was in the same flight with someone who in the world of rugby was already making a name for himself and was to become Welsh Rugby Captain – Bleddyn William.

The treatment received at ACRC came as a shock to many and they were told there was worse to come when they got to ITW. Initially there were the haircuts (or shaves!) and inoculations – then there was floor scrubbing so their arms did not get stiff, or so they were told, and swimming at the Seymour Hall Baths. It was winter so they had to march down to the baths in the dark (Was it six in the morning? If it wasn't it seemed like it.) with one lad carrying a red lamp at the rear to help any traffic miss them.

Under a new rule all aircrew were supposed to be able to swim one hundred yards and of course they had to be prepared to deal with ditching in water for which the RAF had devised a drill. Dinghy Drill was to become familiar to all both at ACRC and at ITW, and many was the laugh one had, Dad said, when being introduced to it. He told me that in those days not so many young people learnt to swim as do nowadays and for some it was their first visit to a pool, and certainly not too many had been off diving boards which formed part of the drill when practised in the baths. For the drill Mae Wests were used and since there were never enough to go round some had to put them on ringing wet and then climb to the top board one behind the other and await the word of command from the NCO taking the drill.

'Number 1 ready – Jump! Number 2 ready – Jump!' and so on. Dad said that the laughs came from the positions in which some of the boys arrived back at the surface. Once surfacing one had to swim to a Fighter Dinghy and pull oneself aboard, tumble off back into the water and swim to a big Bomber Dinghy and haul oneself aboard and await there until the dinghy was full, say five men, and then on the word of command tumble back into the water and swim to the side of the pool. At some ITWs the drill was carried out from the sea walls or a suitable jetty and could be quite hairy.

Then there was the marching up and down and all around the local streets, and the banging of feet at the halt, and of course the inevitable awkward lad who could not keep in step or, particularly when shouted at, managed to march with his left arm moving out with his left leg – it was quite a laugh really if you didn't take it too seriously, Dad said. Then there was Christmas dinner in the zoo – most of the animals having been moved out of London, probably to Whipsnade, to avoid them escaping should the Zoo be bombed. The RAF had taken over the restaurant.

Dad recalled with some pleasure one particular incident that happened whilst at ACRC. One evening someone came shouting along the fourth floor corridor of the building in which Dad was billeted, saying, AC2 Moggs to report to the Commanding Officer. Dad says he was somewhat apprehensive wondering what on earth it could be – as far as he knew he had never even seen the CO. However, he found the office and knocking on the door went in coming to attention in front of the CO, who was seated behind his desk, saluted and gave his name and last three. As he saluted he saw out of the corner of his eye another officer sitting in a raincoat looking at him and grinning – it was his old pal Del who had been in the RAF for about two years and was a bomber pilot. (Del had been Dad's most constant companion prior to his going in the services and they had had many good times together.) It seems that having a spot of leave Del had come along to get Dad off for the evening so that they could paint the town red – thus armed with a late-night pass Dad and friend proceeded to do just this. Before leaving the building Dad suggested that they went upstairs to see the lads in Dad's flight, many of whom were quite young and feeling pretty depressed – Del was quite an extrovert, unworried by authority and Dad guessed would be a tonic to the youngsters having been through it all before. When Del and Dad entered the billet everyone jumped to attention but Del quickly put them at their ease and they were all soon chatting away and asking questions. Del told them not to worry about what was happening now and that, although most of the NCOs appeared to be right bastards, they were only doing their job and that some were actually human. Del had the previous night been over the Alps to bomb Genoa and, typical of aircrew on active service, didn't give a damn for anyone – he undoubtedly enjoyed telling his stories and so did the lads hearing them. Dad says he is sure that Del's visit made a lot of difference and he is sure he noticed a more devil-may-care attitude in their work than there had been previously. Dad never told me where he went that night, I doubt if he remembers, but I bet he had a headache next morning.

The weeks at ACRC soon went by. He spent his twenty-first birthday on guard duty outside one of the blocks of flats, but living in London he was able to get home one or twice and entertained at home one of the lads who lived in Wales.

He managed to see his fiancée who came down from Bedfordshire the weekend before his posting to ITW (Initial Training Wing) at Babbacombe, in Devon, and had to say good-bye to a number of the friends he had made at ACRC as the postings were spread around. In particular he remembered Bleddyn Williams was posted to ITW Cambridge, so, Dad understood, he could play for the University – yes sport made quite a difference for some. The next time Dad was to hear of

Bleddyn was nearly two years later when in the Officers' Mess of a station in Canada he spotted a photograph of him in a magazine, he thinks the *Tatler*; the caption read, 'Pilot Officer Bleddyn Williams with Air Marshal . . .' – yes sport helped you meet the right people!

He recalled his posting to Babbacombe with some obvious satisfaction; he did not remember marching to Paddington to board the train but he certainly remembered his arrival in Torquay. During the 'phoney war' you may remember he had briefly visited Torquay on his cycling holiday which had been his only previous visit – anyway then it had been like peacetime, well almost, and since then there had been Dunkirk, the Battle of Britain and the Blitz on London, which Dad had lived through. It would be different now, he thought.

They arrived at Torquay station on a brilliantly sunny afternoon; the tropical plants in and around the station made it seem he was in a foreign land, and after the drabness of war-torn London it was like paradise – no it was not different.

Even the barking sergeant who met them ordering them to get fell in with full packs could not spoil that feeling of well-being that Dad says he experienced that day. For those of you who know Torquay the back street route to Babbacombe is quite a climb and Dad says the sweat was pouring off him and his comrades by the time they were halted outside Oswalds and Oswalds Annex which was to be his home for the next few months.

'It was,' Dad said, 'a day I will never forget; it was indeed another world from London.'

Dad can't remember how many flights there were in Babbacombe but it seems all the hotels along the front and many behind were taken over by the RAF. Some were sleeping quarters only, some Officers' or Sergeants' messes, some classrooms, offices, and of course the orderly room. Dad says Torquay and Paignton were the same; there were hundreds of airmen to be seen about the area with white flashes in their caps which indicated they were in training for aircrew. Dad said the RAF had taken over most of the spare hotel accommodation in large seaside resorts and coincidentally come to the rescue of owners who in wartime would otherwise have had largely empty buildings – other resorts were Blackpool, Scarborough, Newquay, etc.

During the next few months they were put through a concentrated course on ground work, including, Theory of Flight, Engines, Navigation, Meteorology, Aircraft Recognition, Morse Code (including Aldis Lamp) and of course plenty of square- (actually street-) bashing, P.T. and sport.

Torquay.

Although Dad didn't play much football while there he did play a game on Torquay's ground, Plainmoor.

He also played on the beach and well remembers one occasion when someone kicked the ball part way up the cliff and it stuck there. Of course there was a general rush from some of the lads to climb up and get the ball, and Dad said he was in front and climbing up, knocked the ball off the ledge and immediately slipped and slid down the cliff with his knees scraping against the cliff face as he fell. His knees were badly cut up and put him out of any physical action for a couple of days.

Apart from course studies, drilling, marching, etc., Dad's course took part in a Wings for Victory Parade through Torquay and then put on a gymnastic display in Dawlish at which Dad's old friend from work, the leader of the band he had worked with, attended, being there on holiday at that time. The latter said he never forgot how the PTI sergeant nearly fell through the platform when it gave way – that was the best part of the show he had said.

Then there were guard duties and two, Dad said, stuck in his mind. One when he was on duty outside the Headquarters building on a lovely late-spring evening when there was a dinner or something in the mess with all the officers and their ladies arriving, and Dad with a rifle having to come to attention time and time again giving the appropriate salute according to rank. He said he was glad when he was relieved.

The second guard duty he remembered was at night. He was sent to guard a garage in the town and as it was pitch black he did as most of the lads did, sat down with his back against a wall. It was about 2 a.m. when he heard someone coming up the road. He jumped to his feet and shouted, 'Halt, who goes there?' and carefully shining his shielded torch in the direction of the person walking saw the man who came across to him. He asked him where he was going and the man said he had just left a young lady and was on his way back to Torquay. Dad checked his Identity Card and let him proceed.

A short while later there were further footsteps along the road and this time, after going through the halt routine, Dad said a policeman came over to him and told him to be on guard as there were rumours that a submarine was dropping spies off along the coast. Dad has often wondered.

Among other memories of Babbacombe were the morning breaks when their sergeant always took them to a little café near the front where you could buy lovely hot rolls and butter – he can still taste them now! Yes, Dad said, it was a different world from London. In the evenings when not on guard duty or fatigues there were of course the cinemas in Torquay and dance halls, plus the station cinema which was in the concert building on the seafront. The views from Babbacombe on a clear day were beautiful and even when running along footpaths or down to the beach with the flight one could enjoy and marvel at the peace and tranquillity.

After being there a few weeks Dad's sister, who wrote letters regularly, informed him that, as she had a few days holiday, she could come down to see him if he could find her accommodation. His sister had worked as a postwoman and in factories throughout the War and was then a factory inspector on, he believed, Sten guns.

Accommodation was arranged through a colleague in his flight who happened to live in Babbacombe and whose mother was happy to have Dad's sister for a few days.

On one Sunday just prior to the due date for the visit of his sister, Dad had put his name down to go with a party visiting Buckfast Abbey with one of the padres. Sunday was generally a free day for aircrew trainees when usually, Dad says, he would go for a walk in the morning with some of the lads ending up at a café on the front – that is after church parade – and in the afternoon go further afield to Torquay or down on the beach at Babbacombe. The trip to Buckfast was on public transport and they had to change buses at Newton Abbot. It was on the return trip when waiting for the bus at Newton Abbot that they were informed that Torquay that afternoon had been bombed – Dad who had been used to bombing in London said it seemed at the time quite unreal that such a place as he had come to know and which seemed quite remote from the war, even though full of hundreds of airmen, should be the object of an attack. Of course it was quite a legitimate target with the training of future RAF aircrew but somehow no-one ever thought it would happen.

It seemed that fifteen or so German fighter-bombers had flown low over the Channel and under the radar screen. They were Focke Wolfe 190s which when seen in the distance had at first been taken to be RAF Typhoons or Tempests which bore them a marked resemblance. Being Sunday there were many RAF personnel on the beaches which unlike many beaches at that time were free of barbed wire. Unfortunately there were a number of casualties as the planes straffed the seafront with machine guns and cannon shells whilst dropping the few bombs they carried. There was no opposition from the air but in Babbacombe at least they came up against gunfire for on the toilet block on the cliff tops the army had mounted a machine gun, probably Dad thought a Lewis or Browning, and a soldier had returned fire all the time the planes flew overhead at nought feet firing their cannon shells into the buildings along

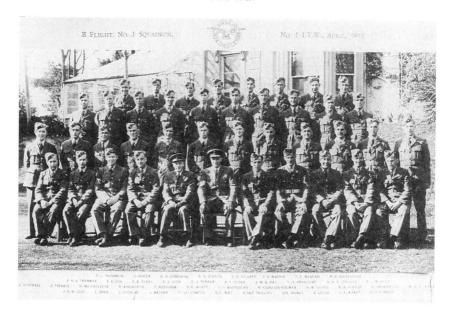

the seafront. Dad says he has forgotten the details but seems to remember there were four airmen killed as well as several civilian casualties including children when he believes they hit the church in St Marychurch. The Wing Headquarters building in Babbacombe was among those badly damaged. Dad remembers that at a dance he went to in St Marychurch a few days later a special mention was made of the soldier who had stuck to his post and fired back at the planes roaring overhead. Whether he hit any Dad does not know but it would be nice to think he did.

Into this mini-chaos (after all Torquay had escaped much bombing) came Dad's sister – after an eight-hour train journey from Paddington. She was greeted with the news that the hotel to which she was to go for instructions as to where to go for her accommodation had been bombed. However, it sorted itself out and Auntie Bobs spent two or three days there.

It was now nearing the course end and there was continued speculation as to where they would be posted for Grading School. Soon the news came – they would be going to Derby (Burnaston). At the course end there were celebrations and parties, and even the dreaded Sergeant Awford showed himself to be a really nice fellow – their sergeant Dad says always tried to make his flight the tops – and it seems he nearly always succeeded; he bred pride amongst the lads and at the 'Halt' the solid cannon noise as 100 feet hit the deck as one was the mark of Sid Awford's men, and all the other flights knew it.

Dad didn't tell me much of what he did in his spare time, whether he made friends with ladies in Torquay he didn't say, but I think he must have known a few, certainly there was one as he told me that when his flight was posted to Derby and they boarded the train at Torquay, he was the only one to have anyone see him off at the station, and I know it was a lady because he told me he was ribbed something awful as the train left. Telling this must have reminded him of something as he suddenly told me that the most popular tune at the time was 'Kalamazoo'.

How they got to the airport from Derby station was a blank in his mind but get there they did and the very next day Dad had his first flight in an aeroplane. It was a Tiger Moth with an open cockpit. From that day on it was circuits and bumps and the many attitudes the aircraft could be put into. The instructor for the first two weeks was a Flight Sergeant and then he was changed over to a young Flying Officer. After seven hours flying, usually each lesson being anything between fifteen and forty-five minutes duration, and some two weeks after the course commenced, Dad was given a test by a Squadron Leader – it lasted about an hour. Dad must have passed.

Most of the lads wanted to try and get approval to solo before leaving Grading School. They had been told that not going solo did not mean they would not be chosen to go ahead with training as a pilot, but most thought it would give them a better chance. All there were either to be Pilots, Navigators, or Air Bombers – it was unusual for those who had been to ITW (i.e., in Dad's case Babbacombe) not to want to be, or at least say they wanted to be, a pilot. About half the course managed to solo. After about eleven hours flying Dad was given a solo test by an independent instructor who after landing told him to taxi to the hangers to let him get out and then told him to do a circuit on his own. Many thousands of pilots have been trained but Dad says he is sure all remember their first solo – not in detail but nearly fifty years on almost as a dream. Nothing untoward happened on the circuit and he landed without mishap, not, however, like another on his course. This individual scared the living daylights out of his instructor and many others by coming in to land no less than thirteen times and flying round again. After six attempts, all flying was stopped and aircraft grounded; the blood wagon (ambulance) and fire engines were brought out on to the tarmac together with the station commanding officer and everyone else who could walk. The young pilot landed at the end of his thirteenth attempt, quite safely after a series of bumps which all who were watching imagined would be the one which would end in tragedy.

The lad said he wasn't frightened but just wanted to make a good landing. Dad doesn't know but was pretty certain this lad was not chosen to be a pilot.

The course at Burnaston ended with a 'twelve-hour test' and before leaving this station they had the usual party which in his case was a night out in nearby Burton (a place then renowned for it's breweries). He remembers nothing of where they went that night but did tell me he remembers four of them stayed the night in a bed-and-breakfast house where there was only one toilet downstairs (probably outside) and that the landlady had provided them with a chamber pot under the bed which when full in the middle of the night was emptied out of the window!

Dad could recall nothing more after this until he reached his next port of call which was Heaton Park, Manchester, then a transit camp for RAF aircrew goings overseas. Again he could not recall how they got there, but he assumed it was by train. Anyway he was somehow billeted with a few others in the top of a large terraced house in Salford. They had a small room where they slept whilst having their meals at Heaton Park, which they got to each day by tram – the fare was three-halfpence. The other two floors in the house were occupied by a Jewish family, who one night gave Dad and his friends tickets to a cinema in Manchester. The key was left under the mat, and one night it was not there and he had to climb up through a window to get in.

Apart from some drill Dad doesn't remember doing much whilst at Heaton Park but after a time they must have been moved to the park itself when he assumes places in the huts there became vacant. He says he used to go dancing at the Mecca ballroom in the city and visited many pubs, some of which seemed to know all too well what was going on. By this Dad meant that all aircrew trainees in Heaton Park were awaiting shipment overseas, which for very good reasons was supposed to be hush-hush. How they knew so much was remarkable particularly as everywhere there were signs saying 'Careless talk costs lives'. Manchester took the biscuit if it were true what Dad was hearing whilst he was there.

He was in Manchester about a month and, apart from the careless talk referred to above, remembered it for going to Maine Road to see the City play United on one Saturday – but not the result – and being confined to barracks one night when he had a date in town. He explained what happened. Why his flight was confined he could not remember but it seems not all in the camp were confined. To get out of the park you had to pass the guardhouse and show your pass but Dad didn't have one. Another way to get out was as a flight with the corporal or sergeant in charge taking responsibility for exit. Thus Dad says he made his way to the camp exit hid in some bushes and waited for the inevitable flight to arrive. He was only there a short time before a flight came marching up the drive and halted waiting for guardhouse clearance. Dad had placed himself near to where the end of the flight would likely be and calling from the bushes got those at the rear to reshuffle their threes and allow him to fall in with them whilst the corporal in charge was talking to those on guard. The flight was then ordered to march and when outside the gate were halted and dismissed. He is sure many others used to escape from Heaton Park in this way – there was never any check made when you returned.

Chapter 7

Shipped Overseas

Eventually the day to move came and the night before Dad was told by a young lady in Manchester that the *Queen Mary* was waiting in the Clyde and that most likely that was where he was heading. Dad then told me that the popular tune at that time was 'Taking a chance on love' and, whereas one hearing a tune often associates with a place or occasion, it was obvious that to Dad Manchester reminded him of that tune.

The train from Manchester went North and yes, hours later they found themselves by the Clyde and were soon being shipped across in tenders from Greenock to the big ship at anchor in the middle of the river – the *Queen Mary*. Later that night the 'Queen' pulled away completely unescorted, relying on her speed to beat submarines. The ship was remarkably empty having a few hundred RAF, a few American and Canadian army personnel, and several British merchant seamen, who it seems were making their way to the west coast of America to pick up newly built Liberty ships – these were 7,000 ton merchant ships which the Americans were building at that time on what was virtually a production line. There were also quite a number of civilians mixed with the officers in the first-class area. Dad learnt on good authority that the ship had just off-loaded 22,000, mostly Americans. In later years Dad was given a book on the *Queen Mary* by my big brother, Stephen, and the highest figure transported was given as 16,000 plus – obviously he says he cannot really doubt the book, but the sailors were so convinced of the number they gave them at that time, he does wonder whether somehow the true number was suppressed, perhaps because it exceeded the limit set. Whatever the true figure, 16 or 20,000, it was a vast number to sail on one ship for over 3,000 miles unescorted in an ocean literally swarming with U-boats. The crew had told them that all the decks were covered with men and that, although every crossing made from west to east was made with a great number of passengers, this particular trip had been the biggest.

The 'Mary' was big and Dad learnt its size the hard way. All RAF personnel who, apart from the crew, appeared to be in the majority on board, were allocated duties to help the running of the ship. Some were put in the galley, some were given police duties primarily to check the ship throughout for possible sabotage, others were given cleaning duties. Dad fell into the last category. His job with several other RAF personnel was to clean the main staircase – the job started at midnight and the staircase had to be swept and swabbed down from the Sun Deck past the Promenade Deck and Main Deck right down to E Deck below. The staircase passed right through the first-class section of the ship.

It should be said that as far as Dad knew the ship zigzagged the whole way across the ocean and having had its stabilising gear removed (or at least that is what everyone said) and guns fitted in the stern, once it started to roll it never seemed to stop. The first night out, Dad said, he felt decidedly queezy and, after an hour or so of deck swabbing starting at midnight, he became ill and was sent back to his bunk to recover – the officer in charge deciding he was likely to make more mess than he was cleaning up. After that first night, which had been very rough, he was OK and carried out his duties every night with the others. It allowed him to see the first-class section of the ship and to marvel at the opulence that must have been before the tragedy of war had occurred.

Rumours abounded on the ship, Dad said: we were going north to near Greenland or we were going south to near the Azores; we were being chased by the *Tirpitz*; a submarine pack had been ordered to lie in wait for us; and Hitler was awarding special medals for those who sank the 'Mary'. In fact the ship must have sailed north as the weather got very cold which of course brought out those pessimists who reminded everyone that there would be danger of icebergs.

After seven days of watching the zigzag wake of the ship or sitting on deck playing cards and looking to the side of the ship and seeing either all sea or all sky in the roll, they were told over the Tannoy that the ship would be shortly entering the waters leading to New York. Those not on duty made their way to the upper decks to see the arrival. Dad says he stood next to an American soldier who previously had never been to New York and soon found himself telling this young man the places of interest they were soon to pass. Dad's best subject at school had been geography and not only had he learnt a lot of New York from films but had many times studied a panoramic view of New York which was the centre-piece of a sixpenny atlas he had bought in Woolworth's before the War. He knew just what to expect: Ellis Island, The Statue of Liberty, The Battery, The Empire State, the Chrysler Building, etc. They eventually tied up on one of the piers where a big American Army band was playing military music to welcome the ship. It was all very exciting and moving: RAF personnel were leaning over the side and yelling down to the band below 'In the Mood, In the Mood, In the Mood' and after one of the Souza marches the band suddenly burst into 'In the Mood', amidst deafening cheers – Dad says the band got a terrific hand at the end.

Dad was a film fanatic, as so many people were pre-war, and through the films he had always wanted to visit New York which had been featured so often, and here he was, right there.

A few piers away from where the 'Mary' was berthed, Dad says, there was a monster ship on its side – it was, they were told, the French liner *Normandie* which had been sabotaged whilst alongside a pier. Men were walking along the hull of the ship but Dad says he cannot remember any more and certainly cannot recall anything since the War which confirmed or otherwise what they had been told.

After watching the band and shouting across to the many dock workers on and in the pier buildings for some time, they were given orders to disembark and form up on the pier. As they got to the end of the gangplank they were met by several ladies handing out drinks, magazines, chocolates, etc. They were treated as heroes and yet, as Dad said, they had done nothing – the people gave them a terrific welcome and it would be a memory he would always cherish. From there they were marched to a ferry-boat which took them across the Hudson to Jersey City where they boarded a waiting train and were soon on their way north. So near and yet so far, Dad said; no stay in New York but straight off to an unknown destination.

The train followed the Hudson River, passed by the big prison, Sing Sing (memories of George Raft) which had featured in so many movies Dad had seen, past West Point, again remembering the cinema, and so on up into New England. They slept overnight on the train and arrived the next day in Moncton, New Brunswick, which was the base for the main RAF transit depot for aircrew for the whole of the Empire Training Scheme in Canada.

They were housed in two-floor huts, of which there were row after row, and the beds were themselves two-tier bunks the type which, Dad says, he slept in for the next year and a half.

He doesn't remember much of what they did whilst they were there; he assumes they had to do a little drill but mostly it was waiting for the day

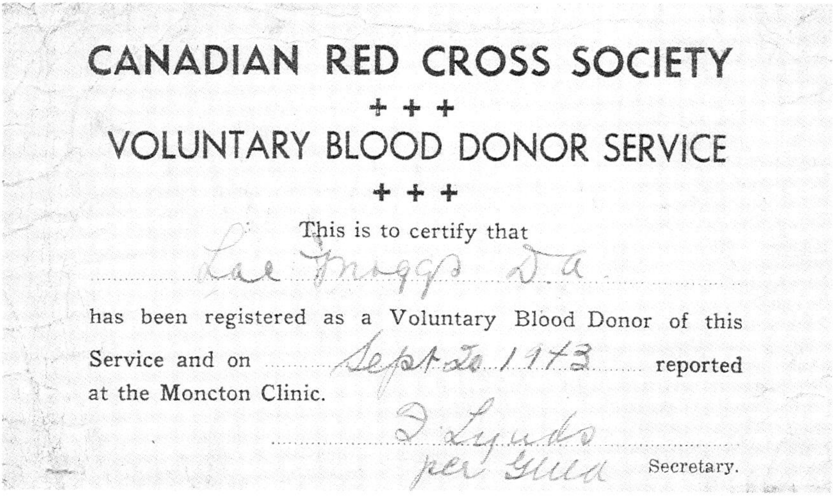

CANADIAN RED CROSS SOCIETY
✝ ✝ ✝
VOLUNTARY BLOOD DONOR SERVICE
✝ ✝ ✝

This is to certify that

(signature)

has been registered as a Voluntary Blood Donor of this
Service and on *(handwritten date)* reported
at the Moncton Clinic.

(signature)

Secretary.

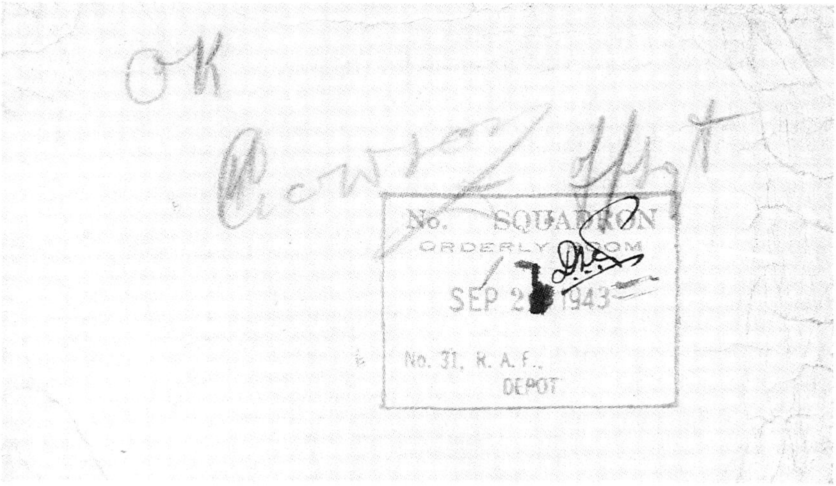

OK

(stamp) No. SQUADRON
ORDERLY ROOM
SEP 2 1943
No. 31, R. A. F.,
DEPOT

orders were received to be moved to an EFTS (Elementary Flying Training School). One day they were indirectly offered a forty-eight hour pass for those who gave a pint of blood for the local hospital – they were not supposed to be told about the forty-eight but it did help to make people's minds up. Dad duly visited the Moncton hospital and on return to camp got his forty-eight. He and another airman went down to St John, the capital of the province. His only memories of St John was going into a public toilet where all the toilets were open without any form of privacy at all, and then being told in the hotel that the room they used had shortly before been used by Walter Pigeon, a well-known film star at the time who Dad thinks must have come from St John.

It was in August when Dad was in Moncton and most were surprised to be warned about the sun, which could cause severe burning. Remember, they were told by the NCO in charge that although Canada, Moncton was on the same latitude as the South of France – it certainly was strange to be warned of sunburn when generally Canada was thought by most people in Britain to be a very cold country.

Apart from going to St John he also remembers taking a young lady by train to a seaside resort which was not at all inspiring – he has forgotten its name and never seemed to remember the names of the young ladies he met; perhaps he was being delicate.

One day in Moncton he met a young fellow from his school days in Enfield who was on his way back to England and civvy street – he had failed aircrew due to airsickness and, having previously been in a reserved occupation in the Post Office, could not be held. People in reserved occupations could it seems get in to the service if they volunteered for aircrew duties or submarine duties, but of course if they failed to make the grade were returned and demobbed from the services. (See letter in Appendix.)

Of course as Dad says there was still a war on but strangely once getting to Canada it all seemed remote and unreal – as yet no mail had arrived from home and although he continued to write it was as if he were writing to people who did not exist; it was entirely another world which was too difficult for him to explain. The locals, who no doubt had got used to the RAF invading their quiet town, seemed to go about their lives as if the strangers from overseas did not exist. Shopkeepers viewed them differently but obtained more money from them when they were in transit back to the UK rather than going west. Remembering back Dad said that, in spite of them being warned of sunburn, his memory of Moncton is all very grey and misty – he knows the sun shone a lot when there, but there was something about the place that made his memories dark.

Chapter 8

Go West Young Man

Eventually the day arrived for them to leave Moncton and, still without knowing exactly where they were going, they boarded a train which headed west. They slept on board in bunk beds which either pulled down from above or were formed from the seats below. Many of the films Dad had seen back at home had included this night-sleeping system which was then used all over North America – curtains were fixed across the sides of the bunks and thus there was complete privacy with a corridor running down the coach between the drawn curtains. The train conductor gave the instructions as to what to do and the same procedure was followed every night.

The train was very slow and the rhythm of the wheels was quite different from those back home and it was some years later that Dad said he realised why – it was simply that much of the track had been welded, whereas back home at that time there was no welding. They were often put into sidings, it was supposed, to allow the transcontinental expresses to pass. They also stopped at a number of remote stations for say half an hour or so, and were allowed to leave the station and visit any shops there might be nearby. It was several days before they reached their destination; they had been along the side of the St Lawrence River; seen the Chateau Frontenac on the other side; passed through Montreal, then the largest city in Canada; and had journeyed north across the wild country north of the Great Lakes. The conductor once pointed out a large Indian settlement and Dad says he was surprised to see how much bigger the wigwams appeared to be compared with those he had remembered seeing in films.

The destination was Winnipeg, capital of the middle prairie province of Manitoba. The platform where they arrived was below ground and when Dad and the many other airmen had disembarked they were ordered to

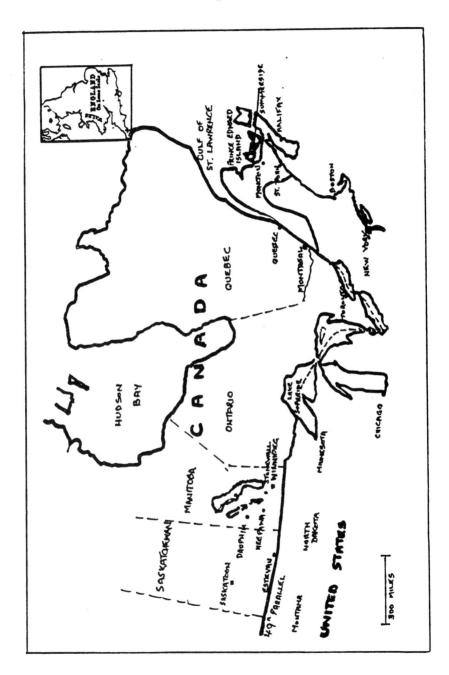

form up and directed to march up a slope to the ground level of the station. Dad says he happened to be near the front and as they started up the slope they saw faces peering over the top. 'Here they come' was heard several times and the unsuspecting airmen lifted their chests and began to march with more purpose. As they broke clear at the top the crowds of people were clapping and cheering – 'Here's the boys – aren't they young', he could hear. The flight was halted and duly dismissed in the main station concourse and almost immediately the waiting people descended upon them. 'Where do you come from?', 'Oh really my Pa came from there', 'What is it like now in the old country?', 'Anytime you are in Winnipeg do look us up.' Dad says he was quite overwhelmed with the friendliness showed to them by these people who had taken the trouble to meet a train loaded with young boys from the Old Country who they realised were no doubt feeling strange and somewhat homesick. Never was that feeling of so much pride to be felt again in quite the same way – Dad says he gets a lump in his throat whenever he thinks of that meeting; the lads, he said, were feeling a bit down after their long journey, from 'Down East' (as the Canadians say), and the utter surprise of such a welcome made it all the more pleasant.

Unfortunately, they were not destined to stay in Winnipeg and, although Dad went back there on leave a number of times, he never met anyone again who had first greeted them, neither did he know of any of his friends who had – but it didn't matter, they had done their job and cheered up the young boys (most were only eighteen) and made one feel welcome to their homeland.

Dad was to learn there were many training schools in Manitoba, some for pilots, some for navigators and some for air-gunners. Their destination was Neepawa, 123 miles on the railway from Winnipeg. At Neepawa they were loaded on to lorries and driven to the drome a mile or so out of town.

Chapter 9

EFTS and Neepawa

Neepawa was a very small town and looked much like a small western town Dad had seen many times in American films. None of the roads out of town were tarmacadamed although they were substantial and well graded. In dry weather a cloud of dust followed every travelling vehicle. There were a few shops and a cinema, and there was a bus out to the camp which was a mile or so outside.

The station at Neepawa was run by the RAF as distinct from the RCAF who had their own stations throughout Canada. Although an RAF station the ground crew were civilians as was the case, he believed, on all stations in Canada. The kites used were Tiger Moths with a difference: instead of the open cockpit Dad had been used to in England, these had canopies so that flying could continue in the cold weather when ground temperatures could fall to forty below and were throughout the winter below freezing.

Before flying again there were some days getting familiar with the course and allocation into flights. Much of a pilot's training is at ground school; in fact an hour's flying a day was considered good. Then of course there were days when the weather was too bad for flying, which Dad said reminded him of his first solo in Canada.

Some months had passed since any of Dad's intake had flown and in consequence all were given a few hours flying instruction before being given the OK to go solo. After a week or so of intensive flying Dad's instructor gave him the thumbs up to fly alone. Dad taxied out to the runway and as he did so an incoming Tiger passed him on his way back to the apron – as he passed the pilot waved Dad back. Feeling a bit apprehensive he turned his kite and taxied back; he half-thought that perhaps he had clamps on his tail plane, which were used to avoid lift when the aircraft was parked. He called over a mechanic and asked him to look around for him – everything was apparently all right. Dad at once again taxied out, did his check at the end of the take-off point and, turning his kite into the wind, revved his engine and moved forward. Just before he was airborne he saw a red flare fired from the tower and instantly he was in cloud. A few seconds later and he was above the cloud and in brilliant sunshine. Of course what had happened was that quite unexpectedly some low cloud had moved in and the pilot waving at him was telling him not to take off; the flare was a similar warning, no doubt the tower having been warned by incoming pilots – but too late for Dad. It has to be remembered that the Tiger carried no navigational aids and no means of talking to the tower. Dad realised that the cloud was virtually on the deck and that it was going to be tricky to get below it – in any case where on earth was the aerodrome. Dad says he turned the aircraft to the left as he would have done to make a circuit of the drome and levelled out at 500 feet. He was he thought up there alone. Suddenly in the distance he saw another Tiger flying low over the cloud and, assuming that any pilot flying up there would know better than him what to do, he increased speed and followed. The aircraft disappeared in cloud and Dad, watching the spot where it had gone through, followed losing height gradually. He was then in the cloud and almost instantly through only fifty or so feet above the ground. He could see the other Tiger well ahead and he followed. The prairie below was very flat but at first there was no sign of the aerodrome. Suddenly there it was, and hopping over the perimeter fence Dad brought his plane in to land on the grass. It was not until afterwards that he fully realised the dangerous situation he had just come through.

Just after Dad told me this I looked at some of the letters from this time and thought it would be interesting for the reader to get a picture of what in the meanwhile was happening back in the UK. There is really no better way than to reproduce a few of the letters written by Betty to my Dad. You will note that the letters are numbered as she did all air letters.

Work whether in school or flying occupied much of the time on camp but whenever there was spare time the lads would catch the bus into town. A favourite was to treat oneself to a T-bone steak or go to a dance which was held in a small hall on Saturdays.

It was in Neepawa that Dad first learnt that many Ukrainians had settled in this part of Canada and many, although born there, found difficulty in speaking English. Dad met one such young lady who, because she had never before left her native village, did not find it easy to talk in English. She had come to Neepawa to visit her sister who had left home and found work in a café in the town. He also learnt that life in these far-flung places

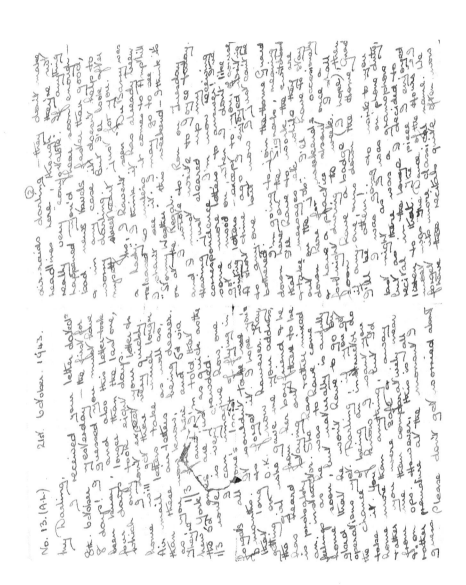

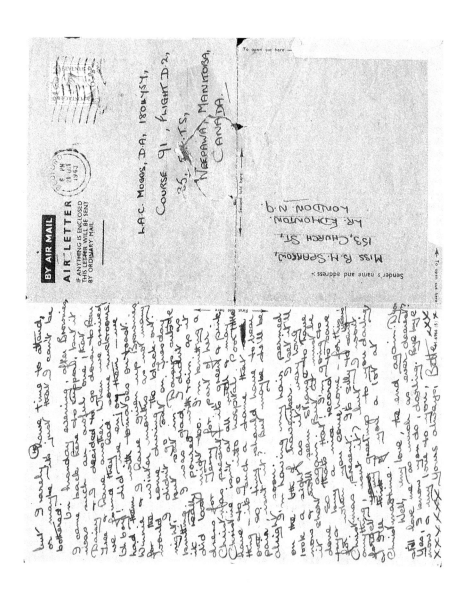

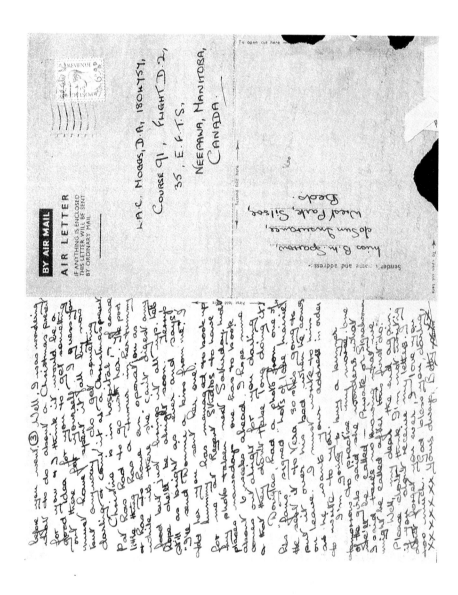

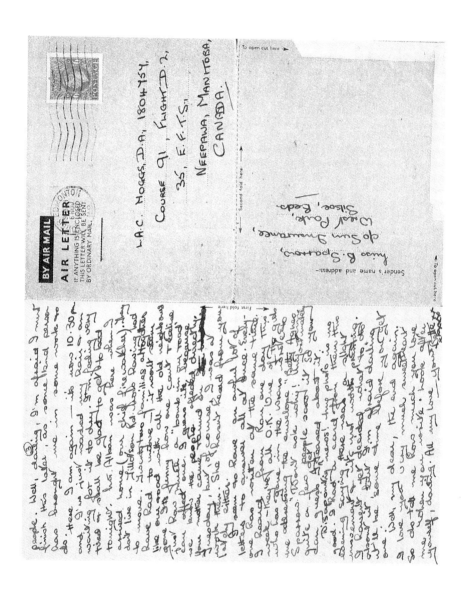

was what girls strove to get away from and many saw their opportunity by marrying men from the forces; hence they homed in on towns near to airforce or army camps. Dad says he later found Winnipeg had scores of young girls who had left home and lived on their own in rented accommodation, sometimes no more than a room under the stairs of a house. It was something that at that time in England was almost unknown, although of course sadly it happened all too frequently today.

Back to flying; Neepawa was the place he first encountered real aerobatics and he well remembers his first solo spin. When you are with an instructor, he said, you know he is going to get you out if you make a mess of something, but when you are on your own it's quite different.

The Tiger Moth does not stall easily and in order to spin you have to stall by bringing the stick back so that the aircraft climbs without throttle; by pulling the stick back farther and farther the aircraft should tip over and spin downwards – you of course apparently flying in a straight line down to a spinning earth. Dad says he made one or two attempts to stall but visualising the aircraft spinning tail first because he seemed to be climbing almost vertically, he levelled off. At the third attempt over she went and pressing hard on the rudder opposite to the spin soon straight-

The Tiger Moth.

ened her out and, pulling back on the stick, came out of the dive. No problem afterwards, Dad says, but that first one was a real test. Looping the loop was easy, he said, but rolls were tricky to control at first. However, his instructor must have thought aerobatics were not his strong point and also he was older than most of those on the course, so at the end of EFTS, if he passed out, he knew he would almost certainly be posted to a twin-engine station for training as a bomber pilot.

Whilst at Neepawa they were given a few long forty-eights and Winnipeg was invariably the goal with a particular house not too far from the centre the best bed and breakfast. The landlady was a very happy and jolly person who always called Dad, Red – he had auburn hair – the place was very popular and always well booked – on occasions they slept three in a bed!

The weeks and forty-eights passed and after a lot of ground school, day and night flying, and solo cross-countries the course came to an end and they were given seven days leave and once again it was off to Winnipeg.

Dad was muddled as to what happened on this leave but he suspects it was the usual round of shops, cinemas, dancing and bars. In one of his letters he recounts his meeting, and subsequent night out, with an old school friend he by chance bumped into in Winnipeg. Les Morgan had passed out as a Navigator and was awaiting a posting back east and thus home – sadly Dad told me Les did not survive the War.

At the end of the leave it was back to Neepawa and on to the next posting. It was the time to say goodbye to those who were chosen for fighter training and sadly also to those who had failed the course.

Coming to the end of the story of Neepawa, Dad suddenly remembered an incident that had happened whilst there and which he said he would be sorry to have missed telling. It seems that one weekend about halfway through the course they were given a forty-eight which he and one other fellow decided to spend in Winnipeg – however, being short of cash they decided to hitchhike, which some other fellows had done some weeks before.

They took the bus into Neepawa and then set off walking along the road which would eventually get them to Winnipeg. It was Friday afternoon and as they walked out of the town the sky was heavy and looked as if it was going to snow, and indeed in the first half an hour a few flakes fell. Two or three cars passed and then one stopped and offered to take them to Portage la Prairie which was a town on the trans-Canada highway, the only road with a tarmacadamed surface. When they arrived in Portage it was already getting dark and they decided that they would get something to eat and then find a cheap place to stay for the night. They went into a small café and ordered some food and were soon talking to the proprietor of the café – he would not take any money from them and offered a room free for the night and on top of that he gave them free tickets to the local cinema, which Dad seems to remember he owned. This all from a stranger they chanced to meet and were never to see again.

The next morning the two lads set off again for Winnipeg. The sky was again very dark and flakes of snow fluttered in front of them as they walked on. This was the main highway across Canada but where were all the cars? The sky got darker and the flakes of snow got bigger – the two airmen put on their balaclava helmets and pulled down the sides over their ears. The flakes grew bigger and bigger and very soon it became difficult to see each other let alone see where they were going. The telegraph wires were no longer visible and the snow got deeper. Dad said they half-thought of turning back to Portage but reckoned they had walked some three or four miles and felt sure there would be some settlement ahead. They plodded on and by now the snow had become so deep that it was becoming difficult to walk. They continued forward convinced that they must soon reach some habitation. At last right in front of them they saw the shadow of some building and they breathed a sigh of relief. When they touched its walls and moved slowly around it they realised it was some sort of shed. They moved round to the other side which offered more protection from the blizzard – Dad said the wind was howling so much that they had to shout to make themselves heard. They were getting very cold and pressed themselves hard against the door to the shed which was locked. They had been there only a few minutes and were considering breaking the lock to get inside when through the darkness they saw a light, and right in front of them there soon appeared a figure who beckoned them to follow. The man pressed forward against the wind and the boys followed close behind. After a few steps the man reached a door which he opened and they were all soon inside with the door closed behind them. It was then that they realised that their rescuer was an Indian and that they were now inside a log cabin. The place was sparsely furnished with a wooden staircase leading from the room to a small landing overlooking it, and Dad said that through the wooden bannisters of the landing they could see the faces of two little children inquisitively looking at the strangers who had come to their house. Their mother was standing by a wooden table that stood in the middle of the room in front of a cooking range where a fire burned. It seems the Indians were most kind and hospitable and gave the lads tea to drink, Indian fashion, Dad said with a smile. Dad says he can't remember much of what was said while they were there but they stayed about three hours until the snowstorm abated and it became light again. It seems they had wandered off the road for about half a mile and had landed up at this Indian's farm. From the window of the house, when the snow stopped, you could see the telegraph poles on the main road and eventually a snow plough appeared followed shortly by one or two cars which was their signal to leave the cabin. Dad has forgotten exactly how they did get into Winnipeg; it's difficult remembering some things after almost fifty years but you can't forget being rescued by Red Indians. Dad said he doesn't remember getting a lift but he does remember riding a freight into Winnipeg on one occasion. It could have been this time but he doesn't remember being with anyone, so he thought they must have been driven in by car.

It seems the memories of Neepawa were mixed: he remembers well skating on the small Whitemud River which was he said such a happy memory, going by bus to the next town or village (Minnedosa) to a hop and getting his first introduction to square dancing, he remembers snow, darkness, the Ukrainian Helen, the first solo in Canada, the loneliness and

Skating on the Whitemud River, Neepawa, Manitoba. (Dad third from right, back row).

unreal feeling of being anywhere that was in the real world, and the night flying when he frightened the living daylights out of a poor instructor. Now, he said, it was all a distant dream and not one person he knew whilst there had he seen since the War.

Dad sat back and thought for a while and I did not interrupt; he was obviously reliving some of his memories. He suddenly looked at me and said, 'Yes, it was another world you know son – quite another world and I wonder sometimes if I dreamed it all.'

Chapter 10

Service Flying Training School (SFTS)

Having finished EFTS the next move for the training of pilots was to move to an SFTS. Pilots are from this stage trained either as potential fighter pilots or as bomber pilots – in the former case they were posted to stations equipped with single-engine aircraft whilst in the latter they were sent to twin-engine stations. Dad, as had been said earlier, was destined to be trained as a bomber pilot and, together with the majority of the Neepawa course, was posted to a station called Estevan in the province of Saskatchewan.

They arrived there after several hours in a slow train – it was bitterly cold. The drome was an RAF station and was situated very close to the American border – the town looked as if it had come straight out of a Western movie. Across the border was the state of North Dakota near to where this state joined Montana, and Dad said he wouldn't have been surprised to see Randolph Scott come riding into town. The latter he told me was then one of the most well-known stars of Westerns and I believe some of his old films turn up now and again on TV.

The kites (the word Dad used to me) used at Estevan were Ansons and the circuit (the word used to describe the area around an aerodrome used by aircraft taking off and straightaway coming back in for a landing) it seemed often took planes over the American border and more than one had come down across there. The local Americans called them 'those big yellow bombers'.

As soon as the Neepawa boys got to Estevan they knew something was not quite right as they were straightaway lumbered with fatigues, and after two or three days learnt that the course which had just finished was now expected to be the last from this station which they were given to understand would be closed. The man who had been handing out the fatigues and doing a lot of shouting was the Station Warrant Officer (equivalent to the Sergeant Major in the Army). Dad and his friends were pretty fed up. Although they were only LACs, as aircrew and on a training course they had got used to being reasonably treated by the officers and NCOs instructing, but now they were being given all sorts of nasty jobs. However, one night soon after learning of the station problem, Dad was in his hut with some of the lads polishing the floor which they had been ordered to do. Polishing, when not under supervision, usually entailed getting a blanket and sitting on it one of the small chaps, or indeed anyone who fancied a ride, and pulling him up and down the room accompanied by much shouting and laughter. Dad who was in the midst of one of the runs suddenly heard his name shouted from the other end of the hut. The corporal who had made himself heard over the din repeated his message, 'LAC Moggs to report immediately to SWO's office.' Of course Dad feared he was going to be given a particularly nasty job as he had seen this man in action.

Dad entered the SWO's office and stood to attention. The SWO looked up, 'Where do you come from in England, lad?' he said.

'Enfield, Middlesex, sir,' Dad replied.

'Is your father's name Bert?'

'Yes sir.'

'Well I'll be damned, I knew your dad at school and was in France with him in the last War. I wondered when I saw your name; never heard of anyone else with that name outside your dad and his family. Your dad was a good sort. Come and see me in the morning and I'll look after you lad.'

Dad said he could hardly believe his luck; thousands of miles from home and meeting up with a friend of his father who was the SWO who was handing out all the fatigues. Although as it turned out they were not to be in Estevan very long, whilst they were there Dad and most of his friends had a very cushy time, thanks to the SWO.

Estevan was very cold at that time of the year, temperatures falling to quite high numbers below zero – it was very necessary to have your ears covered when you left a building. In due time it was confirmed to them that the course was cancelled and that they would have to wait for another posting. The station was to close and the course became an embarrassment to the few left to run the station – it was decided that, rather than have discontented aircrew on a station they were trying to run down, Dad's course be given leave. It should be said that most of the young men could not wait to get into action and any delay, and many they had encountered, was like holding a tinder box close to some gunpowder.

Where to go on leave became the topic. Dad had become friendly with a Canadian on his course who had joined the RAF rather than the RCAF – this lad was nearer Dad's age and had left home before the War and gone down to Los Angeles where he had been working for Technicolor. Bart said he had an aunt living in Los Angeles and that he would try to get her to invite some of them down. At that time the border could not be crossed by RAF personnel unless they had an invitation from someone in the States. Bart offered to telephone and arrange the invitation.

Today, Dad said, it would probably be no big deal to telephone from Saskatchewan to California, but in those days it was different. The lads made their way to town and found a suitable telephone near to the booking office of the railway station, or should it be depot? The telephone to use had a handle that had to be turned to call the operator. Bart started his call with all the lads crowded around him in case in the call he forgot their names. Bearing in mind, Dad said, that this was a remote western-type town which looked as if it had come out of a movie, you can imagine the scene. There was of course no direct dialling and in all probability the operator worked from home in the evenings, not that many people he supposed had telephones, so the number of calls would be small. Having tried several times to get the operator he finally made contact and announced he wanted to make a long distance call to Hollywood, Los Angeles. He said afterwards that there was a stunned silence of disbelief, and he had to repeat it. He said he could have imagined the panic at the other end. The cost of the call was to be transferred to the other end if possible, but Dad doesn't remember whether that was possible or not. Anyway they were told to wait and Bart put down the phone. What seemed ages later the telephone rang and Bart was talking on what he said was a bad line to his aunt and explaining what he wanted her to do – he wanted a telegram with all the names he gave her included in an invitation to stay with her. Not only was the line bad but Bart said it probably didn't help with half Estevan listening, as the lads had suggested could be happening. Los Angeles was 2,000 or so miles from where they were and they had not only to get the invitation but then successfully hitchhike the journey down there.

The days passed by and no telegram arrived, but the day to commence the leave was nearly upon them. They had to do something and the day before the due date for the leave they all decided the telegram was not coming and bought train tickets for Winnipeg. The morning they were leaving for the railway station it arrived! It was not quite what they had wanted – only part of one name (alland) and Dad's name appeared and

Form 6123

CLASS OF SERVICE	SYMBOL
Full-Rate Message	
Day Letter	D L
Night Message	N M
Night Letter	N L

If none of these three symbols appears after the check (number of words) this is a full-rate message. Otherwise its character is indicated by the symbol appearing after the check.

Exclusive Connection
with
WESTERN UNION
TELEGRAPH CO.
Cable Service
to all the World
Money Transferred
by Telegraph

CANADIAN NATIONAL TELEGRAM

W. M. ARMSTRONG, GENERAL MANAGER, TORONTO, ONT.

STANDARD TIME

YA9NM

Los Angeles Calif Dec 18 1943

Allen Moggs

RAF 184857 SSPS 38 Estevan

Like to have you and Ellund Moggs for Christmas

Margaret Lynn

1053A19

DELIVER OR PHONE 87 FOR MESSENGER

whether it would have been sufficient to get past the authorities as an invitation was questionable. However, it was too late. I have reprinted the telegram.

So it was the train to Winnipeg where they went to the same place as they had on their last forty-eight from Neepawa. Here they had bed and breakfast.

Came Christmas morning and the lads found themselves in the Airmen's Club in Winnipeg. It was like a morgue that morning – just a few airmen looking lost and perhaps feeling sorry for themselves. It was bitterly cold outside and the streets were deserted. Dad and his two friends played snooker and talked. Ray was from Manchester, and Bill from London. At about 12.30 a man came into the club and asked if there were two English boys in the club who would like to go out to a family for Christmas Dinner. The few others in the club were Canadians and Dad and his friends were the only ones eligible for the visit. However, the family wanted two and they were three – they told him they would not split up and the man, who turned out to be a taxi-driver, told them all to come along as he was pretty certain the family could make space for one more. So off they went to what turned out to be a small very English town some twenty-three miles north of Winnipeg, called Stonewall.

Mr Hutson was the town bank manager and, Dad thinks, Mayor and he and his wife lived in the middle of town – well hardly a town, more like a village. The boys were royally entertained in the Hutson's modest home and were asked to stay over for a few days. They were shown around and taken into the general store where many of the locals congregated around a blazing log fire set in the middle of the store. One of the 'old timers', who looked as if he had lived in the wilds all his life, asked where Dad was from, and much to Dad's surprise said that he had come from Enfield too, and Dad says he knew well the road the man had lived in when young.

On Christmas night they all called at the neighbour's house – the town's doctor, a Dr Evelyn. He and his wife like most of the people in Stonewall

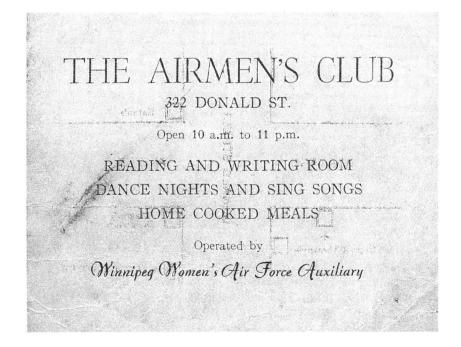

Christmas in Stonewall, Manitoba.

had left the old country many years earlier and the Doctor was very proud of the fact that he was a direct descendant of John Evelyn the writer who was a contemporary of Pepys and like the latter kept a diary which when published contributed greatly to our knowledge of England in the seventeenth century.

The lads spent Boxing morning chopping wood for the basement boiler which heated the house throughout by a system of airducts covered by brass gratings in each room. Central heating was unknown to Dad at that time and he knew of no houses in England which could boast such a luxury – mind you he said with temperatures capable of reaching forty below you needed plenty of warmth.

They enjoyed their stay in Stonewall but, apart from some curling, it seemed most Canadian small towns had their own skating-rink and children grew up on skates, and, paying a visit to look at the local snow-bound golf course, there was really not much to do and knowing they would soon be bored they decided to go back to Winnipeg for the rest of their leave. Dad was to go back again to Stonewall before he left the West and indeed Mr Hutson was entertained many years later in Dad's home in

England – sadly not with the first Mrs Hutson who had died a few years after the War.

Back in Winnipeg Dad and his two friends enjoyed themselves in different ways although all three did spend time in saloons. These were quite unlike pubs back home, Dad said, more like western saloons seen in films, and they sold beer only in half-pint glasses, and customers sat at round tables in bare surroundings drinking themselves silly. The bar waiter collected the price of the beer in something like a bus conductor's ticket machine; it was all very clinical. To buy liquor you had to have a liquor licence and the liquor could only be consumed in your hotel room or at home.

Dad, when he wasn't going around the shops in the day or visiting bars, was for the rest of the leave to be found in the company of a young lady he had met at a Christmas Eve dance. He was taken round to her home and met her parents and brother – the latter an officer in the RCAF. He went skating with the young lady on the Red River – he couldn't remember her name but says he met her when she was collecting for some charity at the Christmas dance. Apparently she was a good-looker and was being pestered by all males who she tried to encourage to give generously to the collection. Dad offered his services as 'minder' and accompanied her around the hall – a friendship developed. It seems Dad's ability to intimidate by just being there worked once again.

The leave came to an end and they returned to Estevan and the collection of any mail from home.

Correspondence with home had continued and scores of letters had been written between Betty and Dad, and I see that Dad had sent parcels home to various members of the family, trying to include items which were impossible or hard to get in England. For example, there was a very high value placed on stockings as is amply illustrated in the extract of a letter from Betty where she devotes a whole paragraph showing how upset she was when she tore her stockings.

One other not so pleasant incident occurred at Estevan when Dad was one of a firing party over the grave of a man who had died; whether it was the result of an accident Dad does not remember. Oh yes, Dad said, a number of men were killed whilst in training, but up to this stage no-one Dad knew.

Dad said they were not at all sorry to leave Estevan and looked forward to their new station – Dauphin, back again to Manitoba but this time quite a bit up north. As Dad told me and I have since checked for myself, Manitoba stretches for hundreds of miles north but, because of the ex-

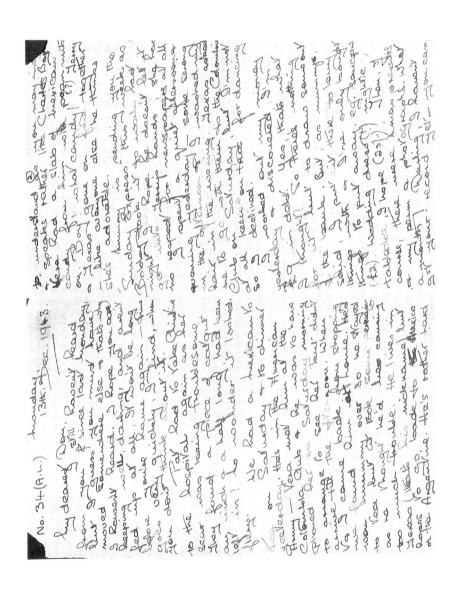

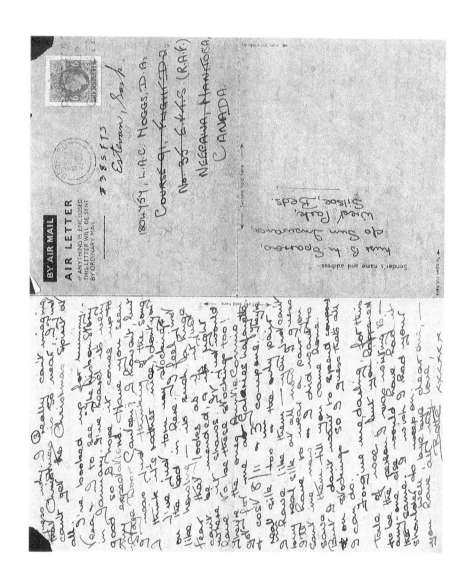

tremes of temperature in this continental climate, the population of this province, the coldest of the prairie provinces being in the centre of the land mass, was nearly all below a line just north of Dauphin, which was some 200 miles from Winnipeg. Maps issued to aircrew at that time showed vast areas of land north of Dauphin as 'uncharted'.

Whether they knew it before they got there Dad couldn't remember but no longer would they be on an RAF station but instead were to be trained on an RCAF station – they believed they were the first full RAF course to be so trained; whether this was true or not they were certainly the first on this station. It was quite different from an RAF station although in appearance it was much the same as other Canadian stations Dad had been on. For one thing you had to salute the flag every time it was passed, and then of course there was the equivalent of the NAAFI – he remembered the vast amount of ice-cream consumed. Then there was the bowling alley and the ice-rink. The latter was an outdoor rink and only for use in the winter when temperatures seldom, if ever, went above freezing – it was floodlit.

His first impression of Dauphin was not favourable; they had had a twenty-four hour train journey in which they had had hardly any sleep and were shipped out to the relief drome five miles out of town with no

S.F.T.S. Dauphin, Manitoba.

Out to R.I. Dauphin.

transport to go anywhere. Add to this that rumours persisted that the
English were not liked by the Canadians and that it was now policy, since
the RAF were now inundated with aircrew, to 'wash-out' fifty per cent of
the course and you can see it did not seem to be the best of postings. The
extract form one of Dad's letters sums up the general feeling – happily
apart from the wash-outs, which proved almost true, the Dauphin posting
did not prove to be half as bad as at first imagined.

All the instructors of course were Canadians and the Commanding
Officer made them feel welcome with a talk he gave them – it seems he
had been in England in the First World War and had been treated so well
whilst there that he meant to repay the kindness shown to him. This was
quite a plus for the course as many of the Canadian airmen previously met

13ª Jan. '44

My dear Betty,

    Well I'm at Dauphin now — I'll warn you before you read any farther that this letter will in all probability be one long moan. We left Estevan early morning on the 11ª & arrived at Dauphin 24 hrs. later after no sleep to speak of — we were messed around all day & finally bundled out to the relief landing ground about four or five miles the other side of town — we're going to stick here for at least two weeks awaiting our course. We've heard some pretty bad news about this station — as you know by the address it is a Canadian station (I mean R.C.A.F.). Apparently they don't like English fellows — out of one course of men in which there were eight home country boys only one passed. That's more than a coincidence for me. So I'm quite expecting to be washed out as a pilot soon after we start — not that it bothers me particularly, it annoys me more than anything. They have spent hundreds of pounds on getting us so far & now they seemingly will be washing over half of us out & yet they keep us hanging around waiting. Canadians who joined the R.C.A.F. months & months after I did already have their wings — its not right & they keep on asking for volunteers for air-crew, they don't even know what to do with what they've got. I'm fed up with it all — some of the boys are seriously thinking of asking to be transferred to the Army, — I know I wish I'd never come in this racket, its been one mess up after another ever since I came in — no-one seems to know anything about what is going to happen ever. No kidding all these boys here were itching once to go on operations but they openly admit that any keenness they did have has been knocked out of them ages ago, & this messing about isn't improving things. From this camp there is no transport into town so you can imagine how often I'll walk five miles each way — I've never been so fed up in my life — if America wants Canada she can have it!

    Sorry about the above but it might help me a little if I blow off a little steam —— when I came back from leave I received a whole pile of letters including five from you, thankyou darling. Oh

20ª January 1944.

I have only received 3 letters in over a week since coming here — one from you darling, one from Babs & one from your Mother — I'm very pleased that your Mother got my parcel O.K. & I'll be replying to her letter shortly. One of my parcels has still not arrived, the one for Babs —— I have sent 5 altogether since I came to Canada — 2 to you (which have arrived) 1 to my Mother & one to yours (which also have arrived) & 1 to Babs.

We had an advance of pay to-day as everybody is broke — they gave us a monthly 5 $ & we had a 48 hr. pass this week-end too. I was going to Neepawa but I don't think I shall now. I have been up flying here now — it is the first time I have ever been in a twin engine kite, my instructor is a young Canadian, a nice fellow I think — each instr. has 4 pupils & we are his first pupils since he became an instructor. When at Neepawa my instructor was new also, so I seem to pick the same each time. These are very nice kites & I hope I'll be able to get along with them O.K. — there is plenty to learn in them — there is one big host of instruments in front of you — you sit at the instructors side & instead of a joy stick as in single engine kites you have a wheel — they are much faster & 150 m.p.h. is quite easy to reach. I like them very much

The weather is very strange — the temp. during the last few days has gone right up above freezing & there was actually some rain to-day the first I have seen for months — infact since we came to Manitoba at the beginning of Oct. last I believe it has only rained once before. Incidently your photographs were the first to have been received by me which were addressed direct to Estevan — so it won't be much longer now before you are writing direct to me here at Dauphin.

had not been too friendly towards the RAF – there was obviously going to be a fair amount of friction to overcome even though they put several Canadians on the same course. With respect to this, Dad says it soon was to be obvious that the Canadians were not, on average, up to the standard of the RAF on ground school work but on average were better than the RAF in the actual flying – they flew more by the seat of their pants, Dad said. He believed that the superiority of the RAF in ground school resulted from the fact that the UK practised an elitist form of education in their Grammar and Public Schools. He doubted whether the present UK education would now prove in any way superior, except for the Public schools and the few remaining Grammar schools.

The friction between Canadians and the RAF was not helped by what seemed to be the general preference of the Canadian equivalent of the WAAFS, i.e., the Womens Division (WDs) for the men of the RAF.

It was at this point that I interrupted. 'Dad ,' I said, 'you've told me a lot about the station but didn't you go there to fly. What about that? What planes did you fly?'

'Well son,' he said, 'when you look back fifty years certain things stick in your mind and these are just as important as the flying, although at the time flying of course was what it was all about.' He went on to say, however, that ninety per cent of work time was ground work and only ten per cent flying – there was Navigation, Meteorology, Armaments, Theory of Flight, Engines, Aircraft Recognition, etc., all to be coped with at school and the ten per cent flying covered both day and night flying, low-level flying, forced landings, formation flying, etc.

The planes used were Cessna Cranes or Bobcats as they were called in the States. They were twin-engined aircraft capable of just over 200 m.p.h. For beam work, that is SBA (Standard Beam Approach) which was then the system for being guided to a landing, usually at night, Dad said they used the well-tried Avro Anson.

It was on SBA that Dad said he twice had problems with the same instructor. On the first occasion he was night flying when, whilst turning to get onto the beam, they both noticed a smell of burning and the instructor decided they should call it a day and head back for the drome. The smell got stronger and when they got down, which they did quite safely, it was found there had been a small fire in one of the engines. This of course was all in the game but a few days later, when flying in daylight with the same instructor, some miles from Dauphin the port engine of the Anson they were flying really caught fire. Dad says he was flying at the time and, on the instructor's order, shut down the engine and let the

instructor take over. They headed back towards the drome – they were not in radio contact with the drome but, as they made their ponderous way back with smoke pouring from the engine, it was seen from the ground, and when they came in to land, omitting any circuit before landing, Dad said he could clearly see scores of people standing on the tarmac with fire-engines and the blood wagon at the ready. They landed without mishap but the instructor said he would never fly with Dad again as he thought he was a jinx. Dad said he could not remember whether he ever did or not.

Meanwhile back in England life continued much as before. The spasmodic bombing of London continued, and from Dad's letters I can see he worried, and with good reason when one reads some of Betty's letters of the time.

The course soon had it's 'casualties' and reading Dad's letters home he lost a number of good friends who did not make the grade, no doubt simply because the instructors had been told to pass only the very best. Earlier in the War they could not afford to be so fussy and, although in no

10ᵗ February 1944.

My dear Bette,

They have started washing out already, my pal Jock Kirk is off & I believe a couple of others will be also ——— also some more bad news to-day. We understand that even if we do stay on, the course has been extended by 4 weeks, so darling it doesn't finish until halfway through June — oh dear it seems that someone doesn't want me to see you too much. Do you realise darling that we have been apart a lot longer then together — when I first took you home I found that

1804757 LAC MOGGS. D.,
Co. 99
No. 10. S. F.T. S.
DAUPHIN,
MANITOBA.
CANADA.
13 . 2 . 44

My dearest beloved,

Today is Sunday & we aren't flying. from now
on we won't be flying on Sundays as the course has been extended to 20
weeks. I am sitting on my bed & there is a terrible racket going on — some
of the boys are singing! — its most distracting cos I find my self singing
with them. It has been snowing again — we having some quite bad
weather now, still in a couple of months it should begin to get warmer.
I don't know how much longer I'll be here — next week there is going
to be a big washout — I'm hoping against hope that I won't be singled
out. My pal Tom is up for the 'washing machine' On Monday with the
C.F.I. — gosh I hope he makes it & I'm keeping my fingers crossed that
I don't get one.

Haven't heard from you since Thursday when
I received an Air Letter which was held up somewhere. How are you

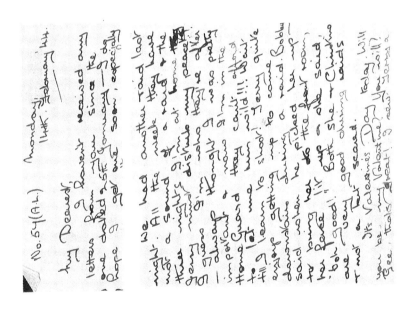

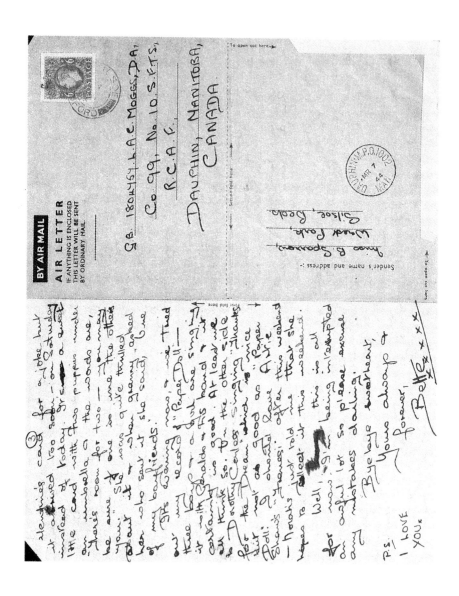

17ᵗʰ February 1944.

My dear Betty,

I received another Air letter from you to-day darling — thankyou it was very nice & I was especially pleased as in it you say that George has been taken off of the seriously ill list — thats certainly some good news, I hope he continues to progress favourably. That last letter is no. 53 so now I have all except 48 & 49 ie. all up to 53 — I expect those two will turn up. I'm glad you were pleased that I liked your photograph & that you liked my letters — I'm afraid that since those two you have received a bad one or two, however theyve got better again havent they dear.

Well I'm pretty tired as usual & so I shall have a pretty early night to-night. I'm certainly pleased we have a 48 this week-end, I need it after all this running around. I have now done 20 hrs. flying at this school so theyre gradually piling up — only 130 more to do — if only I can stay on. A couple more have gone now & our numbers are beginning to thin out — its a terrific strain not knowing whose next, however I have my fingers crossed. I went on a dual cross-country yesterday — we went to Kosmal in Saskatchewan & then to a place called Sunkroats & then back to Base — over 200 miles all together. The last leg was done low flying the whole way — we flew at tree top height (it was quite official so dont think I was breaking regulations) — it was a terrific thrill rushing over the ground at about 150 m.p.h. — boy it was great.

Last evening I went to the camp cinema & saw a very thrilling film "The Uninvited" — Ray Milland & Ruth Hussey, also a very lovely new young lady Cornelia Otis ⸺ (I cant think of the last name). You should see this film if you get a chance, I wish I could see it with you & then you would probably make me hold you ever so tight because its creepy — I'd like that very much, too bad I wont see you for so long. I dont think I shall go anywhere on this 48 — in any case I'm going to send you a parcel so I shall have to do some shopping.

I'm sorry to hear Douglas is going abroad, I hope they change their mind & stay — its no fun being away from home believe me. I hope you have my photographs by now — do you still love me darling? — I love you very much my darling & I'm always thinking of you.

The weather is much the same out here now — occasional snow — when not snowing the sun is always shining but it doesnt give any warmth & its bitterly cold still.

way would they push through a pilot wholly unsuited to flying, it goes without saying they had had to be less severe on standards than was now the case. Men were washed-out for minor taxiing offences and it seemed they were instructed to look out for any excuse to put a person off the course.

As far as the Canadian instructors were concerned there was no apparent animosity towards the RAF boys and their Flight Commander was particularly liked by all. Dad remembered that some months later when the course was well on to the end that this man had given the RAF lads a talk one night on the possibility of them emigrating to Canada – he was particularly concerned that people should emigrate from the old country to counter the growth of the French population which he obviously thought was going to swamp the country.

Dad's letters fill in the background to some of the early days at Dauphin.

My dearest Bette,   22nd February 1944.

I received two air letters from you yesterday — thankyou one numbered 48 & one 54 — I believe I said in my last letter that I received all the missing ones, well my mistake was apparently I hadn't had 48 —— I've checked up now & I find now that I have every air letter you have sent me right up to 54. Its strange how some get held up isn't it. It is in no. 48 that you mention you not feeling too good, I hope that you haven't had any more trouble with food poisoning & that you got over the other pretty quickly. No I don't recall any fellow by the name of Ralph but quite possible I'd know him if I saw him. I'm sorry you were hurt by me inferring you hadn't written — I'm very sorry darling I'm afraid I say things without thinking sometimes, do you forgive me darling? – Thankyou.

Please darling look after yourself in these raids you're having & keep away if possible as long as you can — I don't think they'll last for many weeks so please please be careful. I have just been reading an account of Sat's. raid it seemed pretty heavy. We are starting to practise bombing now so we're getting our hand in.

Reginald Gardiner, Kay Francis, Marsha Hunt etc. are in Wpg. this week, entertaining American troops there —— there is quite a bit about R. G. & apparently he was born in Wimbledon, which is described as a town very near to London "— makes yer laugh don't it!

Yesterday I went on a solo cross-country to Yorkton in Saskatchewan — 111 miles each way — I am the first in our whole course to do a solo cross-country at this stn. Still darling for goodness sake don't think I'm good 'cos it's possible I'll be washed out any day — yes — I hope you win the 2/6 you have bet me — I'll give you £5 as a present if I pass, apart from anything else, including an extra big kiss for being so patient with me.

There was a film on the camp last night but I didn't go as I had already seen it in Neepawa. Tomorrow there is also a film but again I have seen it — too bad. I expect I'll be in bed pretty early, this is a hellish life — still I mustn't moan. How's George now, I hope he is getting along well — of course I don't mind you writing to him in preference to me, he needs all the mail he can get you can rely on that.

1st March 1944
(Wednesday)

My darling,
I haven't had a letter from you for five days now so I have nothing to answer — neither have I any or much news as I haven't done anything of particular interest. At the moment it is snowing heavily. It has been all day so you can imagine there hasn't been any flying. Or at least very little. We have a 48 this week-end so I hope we don't get snowed up here — I'm seriously considering going to Winnipeg this week-end, I shall see. If I liked I could play a game of hockey on Sat. night for the course — there is a big Red Cross drive on all over Canada this week & on Sat. night there is a big Red Cross do at the Dauphin Arena in town — there is a big match on & during the intervals some of our course are going to give the crowd a laugh by playing a R.A.F. course from Paulson (No.) 3.5 & G) at a game of hockey on skates with broom sticks & a football — I've been asked to play

My dearest Bette,

4th March 1944
(Sat.)

Yesterday I had my 35 hour check & apparently did satisfactorily so I'm still on — now my new worry will be night flying — boy I simply must do well at this, we start next week. I had a letter from Les Morgan (who as I told you was at Moncton as a Sgt. Navigator) & apparently he is still in Canada — he has been at Moncton 3 months!! Yes there must be a terrific hold up — he says Mac was there arriving after him but has managed to get sent home on compassionate grounds as his father is ill. Poor old Les fancy being stuck 3 mths. in that place, & he says that he'll probably be there another 3 mths. — bad organisation somewhere. Gosh I hope that when I eventually get to New Brunswick that I don't have to wait that long before I can get home.

As can be seen from an extract of a letter from Betty towards the end of April, Les did get home and was duly married. Sadly he was killed on operations before the War ended.

11th March 1944.
(Saturday)

Hello darling Bette,
I haven't received anymore letters from you — I wish this post would speed up a little. This week-end as I have already said we are on duty watch & thus are confined together with the prospect of doing some rotten job this evening while some go to the pictures & dancing. We were to have had flying last evening but the weather came in so bad that it was cancelled & to-day we haven't any either. A blizzard has been raging all day & has only slightly abated — the snow is getting pretty deep & drifts are forming everywhere, the wind is terribly strong & sometimes its impossible to see more than 5 yds. in front. I crossed from one side of the camp to the other & had to do it in three stages in order to get my breath back & thaw out a little — boy what weather, thank goodness we don't get stuff like this in England. If this doesn't stop soon I don't think there'll be much flying for a few days.
Darling I hope I get a letter from you soon I do miss hearing from you — I don't know what I shall do if I have to come off this course — a couple more have now been washed out & there are now 20 or 21 off out of 60, so you can see our numbers are getting quite thin — its quite a strain darling & if it hadn't have been for you I would never have come as far as I have. It means a great deal to me staying on & I'm doing my darndest to stick it. I've come to the conclusion that after all we the R.A.F. boys have definitely not been treated fairly — I can't grumble yet cos so far I am still on but I feel very sorry for my friends. —

My darling Bette,

24th March 1944.
(Friday)

I received one letter from you yesterday & two to-day also your telegram — thankyou darling for the letters & thankyou very much for the kind words in the cable. I was very sorry to read that Pat's poor baby has died, it's terrible but as you say if she was likely to have repetitions it is best that way I guess — the poor kid must have suffered according to the way you wrote, but don't worry the baby may not have had the mind to realise suffering at that tender age. Please convey to Pat & Bobby my sincere sympathy in their sad loss.

Well darling we have just come off of another wings parade — No.93 this time, there are only one courses in front of us now no 95 (there is no 97 course now). The Polish Consul to Western Canada presented the wings to the boys — there was a fair sprinkling of English lads amongst them, it was a pretty good parade & an Air Marshal introduced our distinguished visitor.

I haven't yet sent that 2nd parcel as I haven't hardly any money — neither have I sent the one to Babs or the one to Mum & Dad, I spent too much money, I haven't been so hard up for a long while now. Tonight I am flying again — at 1.00 a.m. but at 10.30 p.m. I have to report to do duty in the control tower signalling the kites in & out. I have done 4½ hrs solo at night now & tonight should be doing 2 more hours — I hope we fly then we will not have a lot more hours to do at night. Tomorrow we fly all day so I shall be pretty tired on Sat. evening — however I want to go to the dance to-morrow so I hope I'm not too bad. I shall be very glad when next 48 comes — I'm always saying that aren't I darling — I want to get this all over with so as I can come home to marry you.

I'm glad George is getting along O.K., I'm afraid I haven't written yet, I have written hardly any letters lately except to you, honestly darling I owe scores — gosh I wish I could just say presto! & find them all answered.

For those lucky enough to miss 'the chop', flying carried on apace and soon the course were becoming very proficient pilots, and eventually were allowed to fly on low-level cross-country's. This was exciting and the best way of flying, Dad said. They were warned to stay away from mink farms which were clearly marked on maps but apart from that they could fly really low over designated areas. Then there were the straight forward solo cross-country's. One Dad remembers well was to Saskatoon. He remembered it well for two reasons; one for a problem he encountered en route and the other for who he met there.

He took off from Dauphin quite normally about lunch-time having previously worked out his course and studied his maps carefully. Dauphin was just north of Riding Mountain National Park, a vast expanse of forest and lakes which rose to about 5,000 feet. The course to Saskatoon was directly over this park and, as Dad flew gaining height and carefully leaning his mixture to preserve fuel, his port engine suddenly cut out. At that time he was well over the forest and having immediately stopped the aircraft from swinging towards the dead engine, a procedure which had become second nature to him as his instructor was often purposely cutting one of the engines in flight, and having settled down to what had hap-

'*A Flight to Saskatoon*'.

pened, he proceeded to go through the flight checks designed to try to locate such problems. All aircraft were supposed to be able to maintain height on one engine but as he began his check he noticed he was slowly losing height even when he increased throttle on the one good engine. The forest was definitely getting nearer and no sign of anywhere to land – his airspeed was about 180 m.p.h. and the trees below were now moving quite fast beneath the wings as the ground below rose and his aircraft lost height. One of the checks was on the mixture and as Dad increased the mixture on the 'dead' engine it thankfully picked up and with some relief Dad pulled back gently on the control column, and the aircraft began to climb. He realised that in his efforts to preserve fuel he had starved the engine and from then on he made sure he did not overdo 'leaning' the mixture.

He arrived at Saskatoon without further mishap – I should mention that there was no radio control in this aircraft; the only contact with the ground was when one was within sight by using morse on the Aldis lamp. He reported in and found a bed for the night and after a meal he and another colleague, who had arrived from Dauphin soon after him, decided to go into town for the evening. At the bus stop outside the camp Dad was most surprised to see standing there someone he knew. It was the young brother of an old school friend. Cyril was stationed at Saskatoon and was later once again to meet up with Dad. His brother Charlie, who was Dad's age, had been in the services much longer than Dad and had for some time been a pilot in the Fleet Air Arm of the Navy. Sadly, Dad said, he believes Charlie was later killed in the War.

The weeks went by and more and more young men were thrown off the course for what were often quite trivial matters – it was obvious to all that both the RAF and RCAF could be much choosier than they could earlier in the War. Dad said they just didn't want us! Some of the letters Dad wrote to brother Stephen's mother give a pretty good picture of what happened during Dad's stay at Dauphin, and I can think of no better way than to show some extracts. Dad has over fifty letters that he wrote to his fiancée whilst at Dauphin and about an equal number to him from her.

In the early part of his stay in Dauphin there was a covering of snow all over the airport, but the course was to continue right through a hot prairie summer. At this point Dad was reminded of how once he thought he was about to lose his place on the course due to a heavy landing he made on snow. He was flying solo and said it was not easy to judge height when everything below looked the same – he came in to land on his home station and hit the deck rather heavily which he felt sure must have caused

6ᵗʰ April 1944.

My dear Bessie, I haven't had a letter from you for a couple of days now – how are things dear? Well 10 weeks of my course are practically over & we should be finished in about another 7 or 8 – however as I have said before we can't graduate until the full 20 weeks are up. As you can see I am still sticking on the old course – it would be a terrible blow to me to be thrown off now, still I guess I'd just have to take it. I'm well on my way to finish my night flying – I have finished all my night solo time & all that remains now are two more cross-countries & about 3 hours night S.B.A. Last night I acted as 2ⁿᵈ Navigator on a cross-country – the 2ⁿᵈ's job at night is much harder than the 1ˢᵗ – you have to be right on your toes for 3 hours – we went about 300 miles & did it O.K.

The weather is much warmer now & it certainly looks as if Winter is passing – most of the snow has gone & from up aloft it looks entirely different from what we have been seeing for the past few months. The fields however aren't green as in England, still every now & again one can find a patch turning slightly green – you see the snow & intense heat in the summer ruin any chance of the soft green grass of the beautiful English countryside. Yes grass in my opinion is lovely to look at – it reminds me in particular of the lawns at West Park – that is truly soft grass grass isn't it – its only after hundreds of years of cultivation that such a standard can be attained. Gosh I talk of all sorts of silly things to you, don't I – I hope you don't mind darling – I just wander on & on, in fact I never know what I am going to write next – I like writing that way, its more like talking to you – & believe me dear that one of the things I want to do most in the world, my other great wishes are all concerned with you —— so — well you can see that everything I want to do still just says how much I love you.

I had another letter from my uncle in the States – well two in one in fact, one from him & one from my aunt. The letters are both very nice & make it clear that they'd like to see me – apparently their town is quite a popular holiday resort – imagine only the miles to New York – they have even gone so far as to find the exact distance by rail from Winnipeg to their home (via Chicago & New York — 1867 miles – quite a way, eh! I bet it'll cost me a good fare – I imagine however that I'll have to go via Montreal as then my pass back to Hendon would save me a good deal – I'd like to go via the States route – but – well it'll cost about £14.

Tonight is the music club & at the moment I'm waiting for it to start – it is a request programme & I have put in my requests, which are as follows —— "Miserere" (W. Booth & Joan Cross) "When the stars were brightly shining" (sung by Gigli) & "To hear the gentle lark". I hope at least that they play one of my choices.

Tomorrow we thought we were to have the day off as it was Easter Friday – however we are flying & are getting a 72 hr. pass the week afterwards. That'll mean that we will be

25ᵗʰ April 1944.

My darling Bette,

The weather is still much the same — very nice but to-day just a little cooler than the last week. I am still on the course & have now done 110 hrs out of my 150 —— I had my Wings Instrument Check on Saturday, this is the most important test except for the actual clear hood 'wings test'. I passed the instrument check, according to the testing officer, very well — so thats a load off my mind —— I now have only three more tests left, two minor & the major one (i.e. the wings clear hood test), the other two are S.B.A. & camera obscura. We now have nearly 8 weeks to go & as you can see I have 40 hrs more to put in —— all going well we should be finished about 3 weeks early. We have lost two more on the course —— not washed out but just put back one course, that is 4 weeks longer here. One is Ray Kelsall who has been put back through being ill — the other is my pal Cliff Kingsbury, he has been grounded for 3 weeks, given a weeks CB & put back 4 weeks onto course 101. He had a minor taxying accident, he tried to taxy his aircraft between two others but there wasn't enough room & he scraped one of them — they take a very serious view of anything like this & so they clamped down on him very heavily — its too bad, I only hope I don't have any bad luck like that.

I went to a concert on camp on Sunday — it wasn't too bad but could have been a lot better, still they did their best. Last evening we had a soccer game — our course played 105 course & unfortunately they beat us 3-1, it was a very good game — needless to say all the players on both sides were English or Scottish lads. We are playing them again shortly so hope to get our revenge.

After the game, I went to the station cinema & saw an excellent film — at all events it appealed to me — it was one laugh from beginning to end. It was Robert Walker, Donna Reed, Robert Benchley etc. in "See here Private Hargrove".

11ᵗ May 1944.

My dearest Belle,

I haven't written for a couple of days as I have been writing exams. We have finished them to-day & have some of the results — I haven't done too badly so far. Here are my results so far. Aircraft Recognition 100% (we had this two or three weeks ago — about fifteen of us got full marks). Navigation 82½% (I am eighth in the course out of 41) Meteorology 95% (4ᵗʰ in the course out of 41) Armaments 77½% (about 15ᵗʰ in the course). We still have the results of Signals, Airframes, Engines & Airmanship. So so far I am easily in the first ten of the course — I hope I can manage to finish up in the first 15 — I should easily unless I have made a silly mistake in the results yet to come.

Two of the lads have been running a book on who would come top at Ground School — I was placed at 6-1 & had a couple of fellows bet on me. The two fellows I have bet on are out of the running & a couple of outsiders are coming up. It's been great fun — my backers seeing that I get plenty of sleep & didn't work too hard (all in fun of course) — every time somebody went & did an extra bit of swotting at night his odds shortened — the favourite "The Bish" (Bishop) has fault-crossed & is lagging behind.

Well enough of that dear — I have yet the biggest test of all to come, — the "Wings" Test for flying — I'm a little worried but I should manage it — I'll most probably get it to-morrow, if not some time next week — the sooner the better. If I could only get through, I'd have most of my worries over.

I received two air letters from you on Tuesday nos 78 & 79. — gosh they certainly take a long while to reach here now. You haven't actually told me you've seen George but by the way you speak you think you have already told me — maybe it's in the letter you have sent with the size of your third finger. I thought you'd have to pay a little on that stuff as strictly speaking no more that $5 is allowed to be sent — that parcel was valued at about or nearly £2.15.0. — as for the ring well — of course I'll get it & I can always put it on myself, I don't mean wear it on my fingers either.

I'm afraid this letter is pretty scrappy, I am writing it at the Music Club — I guess I'll have to finish it later as I find it hard to concentrate at the moment —

16th May 1944

I still haven't had my "Wings check" but am expecting it any day — I don't mind telling you this waiting is getting me down. I had some pretty good news to day — the final results came out for the ground school examinations & we have been placed in our final positions — The D.A. (that me!) was 5th out of 41, now what do you think of me, not bad eh considering I didn't work too terribly hard. If only I pass my "Wings Check" satisfactorily then I should be very pleased with myself.

Also today I had a letter from Babs — written later than yours & she tells me of the bombing of the hospital — pretty nasty by the look of the paper clipping she sent. I was very relieved to know your home is O.K. — please try & be very careful ~~this~~ ~~careful~~ darling, you are so lovely & mean so much to me.

Yes I saw "His Butlers Sister" some little while ago & enjoyed it very much. So Vera & Douglas are going to get married eh! — boy am I jealous — not nastily though darling - I'm very happy for them but I only wished it were us — oh well it will be one day won't it darling.

It'll be lovely going to the pictures together

20ᵗʰ May 1944.

My dear Bette,
    I had a lovely suprise to-day. I received 3 air letters from you no's 83,84+85 — thanks very much darling. Again they are very nice letters which I enjoyed reading immensely. At the moment I am in our camps Milk Bar where I have been told to work all the evening, you see I'm On Duty Watch this week + we get jobs every night ——— to-night is Saturday + I'm cursing my luck for having picked this worst job on such a night - the other jobs usually only last a little while whereas this one lasts all night. Oh well in a months time I should be a sergeant - I hope. You said you wouldn't mind if I were a sergeant - well in all probability thats what I'll be ——— a course which graduated at a place not far from here had only 7 commissions out of 58 - they were a complete RAF course too - naturally I'm very disappointed after coming 5ᵗʰ in the class, still there is still a faint chance - we shall see.

    The weather has turned a little chilly again + we've had quite a bit of rain —— as a result we didn't fly to-day, I now have just over 15 hrs. to do. Well darling work is calling I guess I'll have to finish this next day — Oh by the way next Friday Mart Kenney is coming to the drome for an evening. Mart Kenney is Canada's number 1 dance band + tours the big cities of Canada — it is quite a privilege for him to come off the beaten track to visit us up here. Au revoir most beautiful girl in the world — I love you dearest - goodnight ×××××××

    It is now Sunday dinner time — I have been to Church + dinner — this afternoon I hope to have a little kick around at football. I managed to get to the dance last evening when I had finished my duty at 11·0p.m. — it didn't finish until 1·30a.m. so I had quite a time there — it wasn't bad, I really had a fight too.

    So you are on radio sets — what ones are you using. We use the ATR5 for our aircraft — nearly all our kites now have radio equipment + we have to be talking all the time - well nearly - its quite good when you get used to it — you have to watch your language though as the radio sets of people in Dauphin can pick it up — I nearly slipped up the other day - I was trying to contact control + suddenly realised I had been using the remote control unit on receive instead of transmit —— I turned to transmit + swore at the same time.

    We are doing formation flying now — three aircraft at a time - its quite interesting, though quite a strain as one must concentrate very hard — I have nine more hours of it to do.

some damage. As he taxied back to the apron he was sure his undercarriage had been broken as the ground seemed to be almost touching his wing tips. He reduced speed almost crawling back to a parking position for the fear of damaging wing tips which he thought must have been only inches from the ground. Having stopped the engines he got out onto the wing and instead of walking off to the ground he found he was well up in the air and realised it had all been an optical illusion – the aircraft was in perfect shape – thankfully no damage. He illustrated how tough the washouts could be when he told me one of his friends had to leave the course because he clipped the wing-tip light of another aircraft when parking.

The evenings on the main camp and when not flying could become quite boring – when not on duty, which I can see from his letters happened quite frequently, he went into town with some of the lads for a drink in a saloon or to have a meal. The camp also had a cinema show every now and again, and the ice-cream on the camp was quite good. Then of course there was old Bart's photographs – these came out at odd intervals for general viewing. Bart was the man who had worked in Hollywood for Technicolor and being a bit of a ladies' man had gathered many photographs of girls in Hollywood whom he claimed to have met – no doubt at that time there were hundreds of beautiful girls there all trying to get into films, or at least get hitched up to someone earning big money in the then most prosperous industry. No-one questioned Bart's stories but Dad said he certainly could tell a good story with the aid of his photos. He said he knew Judy Garland and told his audience of stories concerning such as Paulette Goddard and other big Hollywood names – it always went down well. Later Dad met several lads who did get down to Hollywood and in those days it was rather special. RAF boys often stayed at film stars' houses and Dad seemed to be intrigued by the fact that one boy he met had stayed at the home of Jesse Willard. Who was Jesse Willard? I hear you say, as indeed I asked Dad. Well, it seems the big name in boxing when Dad was a boy was Jack Dempsey – boxing seemed to have more general importance in the twenties and thirties than it has today – and the man he won his title from was a giant cowboy called Jesse Willard.

In spite of the visits to town, the odd concert show, the bowling alley, and the films, there was something missing – regular dances. Dad, who must have fancied himself as a dancer, said the Canadians like the Americans had no idea of how to dance – dancing then was ballroom dancing which, in the large industrial towns in England such as Manchester and London, had reached a high standard. Dad came up with the idea of running a dance class on the camp – he and a friend, who was keen on

No. 10 S.F.T.S
Dauphin

MUSIC CLUB

Thursday
9th August, 1944

26ᵗʰ May 1944.

My dear Betty,

Well here I am once again + this time I got a bit of bad news — believe it or not they have stuck 8 more weeks on the course — yes first we heard that it had happened to the course after us + all after that + we were thanking our lucky stars that we had been spared — when bang we were in it too. We had all the 'gen' read out to us on parade this morning by the C.O. of the station (Group Captain) — the reasons were given as follows — it is considered that there are enough pilots in England doing nothing already + they figure if they hold up for 2 months they'll be able to graduate a few more. The boys are pretty badly hit — imagine it if I'd been on the course previous I'd have been O.K. Actually I have only 10 hrs. more flying to do — having passed everything fairly well — there was almost a revolution on the camp. we apparently are to do some more advanced flying in the extra 8 weeks — advanced formation, low level etc. One fellow had his father coming to see him graduate — he is one of the two Canadians now on our course — his father had had it all arranged, his home is in Toronto + thats over 1500 miles from here — almost as far as from England to Newfoundland. Yes there are a lot of unhappy hearts here to-day — as I have told in previous letters we have had everything arranged for our graduation dinner, we went to town yesterday (sorry Wednesday) + collect our liquor for the party — we are now deciding whether to have a party or not. We are probably arranging a big parade (the boys of 99 I mean) on June 16ᵗʰ — we've arranged for a band + we are going to have a mock "Wings Parade" — you see having passed our wings checks we are strictly speaking entitled to our Wings — why on earth cant they give us them, the band will play the funeral march — I expect the police will intervene if the boys get too bad but I think they'll be better to leave them alone as the boys are plenty mad. The other courses have been hit the same but its not so bad for them as they're mostly Canadians + at least are in their own country — + anyway they havent nearly finished their other course yet. I don't know what you'll think about all this — this is one thing I never counted on — we don't graduate now until August 11ᵗʰ. As I have said before its quite possible I may be kept out here longer for a GR course after graduating, well if that comes up at the end then it looks if like December or next year before I come home. Mum will be very pleased I know but I really had high hopes of seeing you soon — someone must be trying to save me for you. To me it looks as if the invasion day must be near at hand. All sorts of rumours are circulating now — very prominent is that its the Japs for us — I don't mind whom I fight but I would like to come home first. Well dear I know this must make you very angry but I know you'll understand that I cant help it — we were all so much looking forward to having our wings + becoming sergeants or P/o's. I guess it looks as if you'll have to have your holidays alone this year — please yourself though darling I might be home at the beginning of September — if you wouldnt mind waiting until I graduate in August then I dancing, would teach. They got permission and duly put a notice on the board and as he expected no male Canadians turned up but plenty of WDs – the equivalent of WAAFs. There was this blond lady Dad happened to mention who danced quite well and she became his partner. How many classes were held Dad doesn't remember but he said it went down well with the RAF boys and the WDs.

Another innovation at the camp was the introduction of a music class run by a Canadian officer. Dad said he really enjoyed these classes particularly as the officer was well versed in music and made interesting comments on each record – the music was of course on seventy-eights as in fact it was for the dance classes. Dad had always liked serious music but, although he had a number of good records in his own collection at home, he had not until then a great knowledge of the composers and when and why they wrote what they did. The class numbered about a dozen, boys and girls, and most sat on the floor near the gramophone or fire – the officer himself seated near his machine. 'It was one of my most pleasant memories of Dauphin,' he said.

Winter turned to summer and all had to change into khaki drill – yes the cold prairies in winter turn baking hot and dry in the summer with temperatures reaching the nineties.

The course went on with friends failing to make the grade – there was also some football, played in the summer because of snow, etc., in the winter, and Dad played for the station team and played teams all over Manitoba and Saskatchewan. They flew to away matches, generally in Ansons. He doesn't remember being beaten, although they probably were and I have read a newspaper cutting (the *Dauphin Herald*) in which Dad is given a good write-up for a goal he scored in one home game.

The letter extracts show how time to graduation was counted down and how the Canadians on the course were inviting parents to attend the ceremony, some to travel a couple of thousand miles, when suddenly a bombshell was dropped – the course was to be extended; initially postponed indefinitely.

Dad says you can imagine the mood of the men. It is a wonder there wasn't a riot – instead they sent the course out to RI (the remote relief drome miles outside town) where there was not much to do except fly. The instructors admitted that they had little more they could teach them until someone came up with the idea of nine-plane formation! For those who have flown aircraft with a top speed of 200 m.p.h. and a stalling period of say seventy know the problem of trying to keep formation in a 180 degree turn with nine aircraft in a V formation. The outside plane is at full

Dear Don, I had intended to await your
return from Canada & then to tender my apologies & thanks myself on your relay, our
friends across the sea, had I regret to say, other
ideas. On my last leave I had a feeling it
had reached my alloted span & intended
to transmit my apologies via Babs whom I
saw at St Stephen's with your mother, but as
it seemed unduly morbid so I, unfortunately, here I am, the pitcher went to
the well once too often. I haven't as yet settled
down very well, life seems very strange, I just
managed to get out after my crew with half the
post side of the kite alight & most of the tail
plane otherwise engaged, then I had fun for
a few days trying to walk home from the
middle of the Reich, not to be recommended
in January without food, I was almost glad
when I was caught but had I realised just
how deadly this life in a ███ yard square
of barbed wire can be I'd have died of star-
vation. My regards to your folks, Babs &
all, ███████████████████ would
have liked to have been there. Regards to Bill
Erickson, glad etc. Rowes me a letter. Del.

throttle whilst the inside one is near to stalling and wondering if the one above is going to hold on to his position or come crashing down from above. It was hairy to say the least, and often planes were obliged to leave the formation. It was new to the instructors and new to the students but, like all things, it was mastered, and they did finally get it down to a fine art and it was good fun. Talking of formation flying reminded Dad of one of his course who had been an air-gunner with, Dad seems to remember, two tours of ops to his name; he was already an officer and had remustered to train as a pilot. Dad said, 'He was a mad bugger when flying and would close in bringing his wing immediately behind your aircraft with his propellor looking as if it would, with the slightest movement, chop into the trailing edge of your wing – he graduated OK. He of course lived in the officers' quarters – good luck to him. Anyone who had done a tour as an airgunner and remustered deserved good treatment. I wonder if he survived the War?'

The course had been extended due to the build-up of shipping in Europe prior to the second front being opened, and there was no shipping space available to take trained aircrew back to the UK.

It was whilst at Dauphin that Dad received news from home that his friend Del had been shot down over Germany and taken prisoner. He actually had been reported missing some time before Dad's folks let him know – they only did so when they knew he was safe. They forwarded the POW letter opposite and below is a photo of Del taken from the local paper in Enfield.

F/O ILLINGWORTH

In last week's "Gazette" it was reported that Mr. and Mrs. Illingworth, of Harman Road, Enfield, had been relieved of anxiety by the receipt of an official intimation that their son F/O Illingworth, after having been reported missing after a flight over Germany, was now known to be a prisoner of war in Germany. F/O Illingworth has taken part in sixty operations over enemy territory, sixteen as a member of a Pathfinder crew.

As the weather got warmer 99 course and the rest of the station had to change to khaki drill uniforms – the long hot summer of the prairie provinces, Dad said, proved to be just that. The fine weather helped the men overcome their disappointments and the flying was good, although a bit bumpy at times with the rising heat. The weeks went by and on two occasions Dad says they were able to take forty-eights in the nearby (fifty miles or so) Riding Mountain National Park – the holiday village there was a place called Wasagaming which was next to Clear Lake and the boys went horse riding, cycling and attended the evening singsongs and weeny roast at the lakeside. Dad says he took me there in 1979 and we played football, but I don't remember it at all.

Some of the letters which follow give an account of life at Dauphin right up to Graduation and include reference to the big parade held before the Air Officer Commanding in which Dad says he played an important role. All the officers in the parade were played by airmen and there was plenty of practice to make sure the AOC was duly impressed at the drill.

Unlike Moncton, Dad says, his memories of Dauphin are nearly always bright and, in spite of the initial bad wintry weather and the unfortunate start at the station, he will always remember this station with affection. We visited it, Dad said, but of course it was no longer there, just open prairie and remains of hangers – but I still don't remember a thing; I was not quite four.

'Digging' snow ditches at Dauphin.

A 48 at Clear Lake, Riding Mountain National Park.

My darling Bette,
                     11th June 1944.

       I received another letter from you yesterday, I was going to write to you then but had to go on a special trip. I did in all 6 hrs. 10 mins flying yesterday, which isn't Scotch mist! I did over 3 hrs. bombing in the morning & then they wanted four to go on a trip to Saskatoon — it is a new idea in our new extended course — & I volunteered to go —— it was good fun, two in each aircraft, one acting as pilot & the other as navigator — I was pilot of my ship & we got there O.K. On this trip we had to go via Langenburg so that it wasn't just a straight trip there. We left about 3·15 p.m. & arrived there 2½ hrs. later which was good going — it was 307 mile Saskatoon is together with Regina the largest towns in Saskatchewan, it is the furthest West I have ever been —— we naturally had to stay the night there, the other ship piloted by Doug. Wiltshire although starting 10 mins before us arrived 5 mins after so we must have stepped on it a bit — I had her beating it out at nearly ¾ throttle all the way, it was a nice ship. My navigator was Alec Waton a Yorkshire lad – a very nice fellow —— So together with my navigator & Doug & his navig. we all went into Saskatoon in the evening & had bit of fun. It is a very nice town & the best I've been in in Canada — it is quite large having a population of about 80,000 & straddles the Saskatchewan river which at this point is about ½ a mile wide — being fairly well north the prairie is not so empty & a fair number of forests are found. Except for the mosquitos it is very much like an English town along by the river. To-day we came back, Alec being pilot & I navigator —— again we made pretty good time having to come back a different route, this time ⅞ farther north via a small township called Endeavour. I really enjoyed that trip & only hope we get some more like that, its quite interesting landing a kite on a strange drome.

       Sorry if I've bored you with the above but I have only just come back & so it is on my mind. Well darling the letter I received yesterday morning was no. 92. — as yet I haven't received the letter you wrote thanking me for the parcels but I imagine you sent it via ordinary air mail, I hope so darling, also I'm afraid I'm one air letter short, I do hope it hasn't got lost.

       I do hope Vera & Douglas managed to get married & also I hope that Douglas hasn't had to go to the fighting — I haven't heard the news for a couple of days so I guess I'm not right up to date on the news. Darling your letters are very very nice lately. I hope mine are alright, I do my best darling. I don't know whether I'm doing wrong in asking you but would you like me to get you some material over here for a wedding

23rd June 1944.

My darling Bette,

I haven't written for a couple of days as I have been very busy — I came back from Saskatoon this morning, I went down there again yesterday & flew back to-day. This is the 2-d time I have had to go there on a cross-country & who should I meet there but an Enfield lad — he is a friend of mine. When I was at school I used to be friendly with a fellow called Charlie Lavender who lives near Del — he had two brothers also at the Grammar — Cyril the 2nd brother is a couple of years younger than me & he was Flight Sergeant at the A.T.C. I used to attend. He went to ACRC about 5 weeks before me & I hadn't seen him since —— yes it was him I met at Saskatoon — he is still on the course & like us has had two months stuck on the end — actually he was on course there before I came to Dauphin but was sick & is now on 100 course & so is 2 weeks behind me now. Both of us were very suprised — we went out together in the evening & had quite a good time.

21st July 1944.

My dear Bette,
I haven't written for a couple of days & I'm very sorry believe me but I've been pretty busy flying — yes they have stuck another 20 hrs. onto us & we are struggling to get it finished within the time, its going to be a rush, I now have done 195 hrs. at this school & we were originally intended to do 150 hrs. Yesterday I went on a long solo cross-country, it was very tiring — about 800 miles, from here to Saskatoon via Regina — landing — then to Yorkton via Melfort - landing — back to base — it took all day. actually 6 hrs. in the air which is quite a time when by yourself. To-night I start my 48 at 5.0 p.m. we hope to be off to Clear Lake again — boy I am tired, I've been flying all morning & it looks as if I'll be up again this afternoon — phew I wish I could rest, I can't stop shaking.

How are you now darling? I had a couple of letters from you on Wednesday the first for over a week — thank you very much dear they were very nice. Yes as soon as I get the opportunity I'll try & get Vera some stockings & don't be a silly girl about that money of course I'll give it you, I owe you more than that if I remember correctly. I guess it was rather stupid of me to put that silly sentence about the buzzy-bombs — but I just couldn't put or think of anything else to say about them, yes I think I can realise what it must be like & I sympathise with you — I do wish I could be with you darling — anyway please look after yourself & please please keep away from London as much as possible, I need you a lot, especially for my moral!

The weather here is now very hot — but mustn't grumble as its really very nice, but the air is so terribly dry that it makes your mouth very dry too. Flying is most unpleasant in the afternoons especially when not very high — the air is very very bumpy. Well darling, 3 weeks to-day is the graduation day — at least we all hope so & then maybe at last I'll be a Sgt-Pilot.

Let me see I think its about time you received your photographs from me _____ I do hope that they haven't disappeared too, I guess the parcels are gone forever now — too bad, personally I think they have been stolen, as none of the other fellows have ever lost parcels.

I'm glad you went round to my house again — thankyou so much darling. its very sweet of you to be so

25ᵗ July 1944

My darling Bette,
Boy we are busy right now — I shall be
very glad when the next 7 days are over — sorry darling to
start that way but thats just the way things are. How are
you darling. — I hope you are getting less of the raids now,
& I hope you are quite well in health etc. — you know what
I mean darling, I pray you are safe & well. Life is really
hectic now, we have the A.O.C. (Air Officer Commanding) coming
to the station next Friday & everybody is going mad — its
been like it for 2 or 3 weeks now but things are just getting
really worked up. The air-crew on the station have to put on
a special ceremonial parade for him —— the boys will be
doing everything, acting as officers & N.C-O's. — I am now
acting as a flight Lieutenant for the purposes of this parade
I am flight commander of No.1. flight No.1. Squadron, so you
can see I will be giving the word of command that starts
the parade off — phew & what a parade, march past by
flights, march past by squadrons & march past by Wing
& bags more ceremony. Still its quite good experience for
those who will become officers — no use to me I guess but
still theres always a chance of getting a commission after
being on operations a while — boy I only wish we knew who
was going to get commissions & who not I think I should
have stood a pretty good chance on an RAF station, especially
coming 5ᵗ in the course, but on an RCAF station my chances
are very slim indeed — oh well I shall be satisfied with my
three stripes, I did my best anyway & satisfied myself I
wasn't so bad. To crown things we are on Duty Watch this
week & so are Joed each night —— in the day when we
are not flying we are painting the flight room etc —— in
fact the whole camp is in a turmoil because of one man
visiting the camp, I haven't had a moment to myself
for days now, while on camp.
                    We had a lot more rain to-day & a
couple of bad thunderstorms —— I was forced to land at
Paulson aerodrome as we were unable to get into our
base owing to hail & severe lightning — phew what a
day this has been! We got back from Paulson this afternoon.
                    I had three letters yesterday, two from
Mum which have taken a month to get here, One incidently

REGISTRATION OF CHANGE OF RESIDENCE

Permanent. Valid only when permittee has made application and remitted the fee of fifty cents.

Temporary. Valid only when registered by an authorized officer of the Commission or a Beer Vendor Licensee. No fee required.

Persons wishing to obtain permits must be over twenty - one years of age.

It is required by law that your permit be produced and particulars of your order endorsed therein when purchasing liquor.

It is contrary to law to consume liquor purchased under the authority of this permit in other than your residence, the full address of which must be contained in your permit.

FORM NO. 15—28-A   REVISED 1-5-44.

"THE GOVERNMENT LIQUOR CONTROL ACT, 1928"
R.S.M. 1940
GENERAL PERMIT Expires April 30th, 1945.

No. **11 S 4201**

This is to certify that the person whose signature and address appear below has made application in the prescribed form and is entitled under General Permit to purchase liquor for beverage, medicinal or culinary purposes in accordance with the provisions of "The Government Liquor Control Act, 1928" R.S.M. 1940, and the regulations made thereunder.

INITIALS		SURNAME						
D	A	M O G G S						

NAME OF PERMITTEE IN BLOCK TYPE LETTERS — IN INK

Issued at .... DAUPHIN, MAN. ...., in the Province of Manitoba.

this .... day of MAY 23 1944 .... A.D. 194........

Signature of Permittee .... *DMoyes* ....

(In Ink)

.... Hut 3 B HIOS. F.T. S. ....

(No.)   (Street)   (City or Town)   (Sec., Tshp. or Range)

Attested—Authorized Officer. 7   W.M.Clubb

                                                    Chairman

MONTH DATE QUANTITY		SPIRITS IN OUNCES									WINE IN OUNCES							BEER IN BOTTLES							
MAY	D	23																							
	Q	26																							
JUNE	D																								
	Q																								
JULY	D	19																							
	Q	12																							
AUG.	D																								
	Q																								
SEPT.	D																								
	Q																								
OCT.	D																								
	Q																								
NOV.	D																								
	Q																								
DEC.	D																								
	Q																								
JAN.	D																								
	Q																								
FEB.	D																								
	Q																								
MARCH	D																								
	Q																								
APRIL	D																								
	Q																								

PERMITS ARE NOT TRANSFERABLE. IT IS A VIOLATION OF THE LAW TO ALLOW ANY OTHER PERSON TO USE YOUR PERMIT.

My dearest Boo,

31st July 1944.
(Monday)

    I had two letters from you to-day darling for which I thank you very much — somehow you seem a little blue, I'm very sorry & I hope you'll cheer up a bit — I do hope that I'll be able to come home soon to make you happy, that is presuming I coming home would make you happy. Not very long to go to my graduation now — one week, next Friday, everybody getting excited & irritable at the same time, I have it's ho to fly now! Tomorrow afternoon we are playing MacDonald at Soccer & have to fly there — on Thursday we are playing an away game again at Gimli. Next Wednesday week we have our graduation party & we are going to go through with it this time whether they extend the course or not. Also on the Tuesday before graduation we have a dance so we shall be quite busy during the next week or so. Also we have a 72 this week-end & I can't make up my mind whether to go to Clear Lake or Winnipeg — still it doesn't bother me particularly all I worry about at the moment is graduation.

    It is now the next morning & I am in the crew-room — sorry I didn't finish last night dear. I went to the camp cinema & unfortunately the film was not 'Pin Up Girl' as I thought but 'The Mask of Dimitrios' with Peter Lorre & Sidney Greenstreet — I didn't think much of it so was pretty disappointed. The rumours are running fast & furious now about leave & postings — gosh what rumours too — duff gen mostly. It looks as if I'm pegged for a GR course, worse luck. I so much wanted to come home — all the boys are kidding me about it & it makes me pretty blue, still its not definite by any means.
    Well darling I want this letter to catch the post so I'll have to finish off now in order to get it posted in time. I'm going to dinner in a minute & after that am going to MacDonald to play football. By the time you get this letter I'll be almost graduating — please remember me on that day at 3.0p.m. — that'll be about 9.0p.m. your time, you should be home by then.
    I'm hoping to collect some mail shortly, however I'm not due for any so I guess I'll be unlucky.
    Once again I'll say cheerio
    Keep smiling darling
    Always in my thoughts
    Don

xxxxxxx   xxxxxx

4" August 1944.

My darling Boo, I'm afraid this letter may make you feel a
little unhappy. I'm sorry darling but I must tell you — we have been
given our postings & unless they are altered during the next week I
won't be coming home yet. I have been selected for a General
Reconnaissance Course — I really wanted a GR course but not out
here — I went to see the flight commander immediately I heard my
posting & asked if he would get it changed for me as nearly everybody
is going home. He gave me a long talk to & advised me not to beef
about it, telling me it was an honour to be picked (there are two of us
out of our flight) & that it had to be a responsible & good person who knew
his gen, particularly at navigation, & thus they wouldn't just change it.
He has told me that I stand a very good chance of getting home after
I have finished it & that it will do me a lot of good in the RAF — he
said he wished he were in my position & hinted that I stand a better
chance of a commission even if I don't get it when I graduate next
week. I feel very down as all my friends except one are going home —
everybody is very happy & all talking of home & the boat — gosh I
have a nasty feeling inside me the whole time. As it stands so far Alan
Wincer (the other fellow on a GR from my flight) & myself have to stay
on this station a week after graduation & then we get 10 days to get to
Prince Edward Island which is about 10 days journey from here — so
we will be spending some leave in New York (I hope). I go to P.E.I on
1st September & the course is about 10 weeks if we start right away.
        Darling I guess you had better have your leave
as I at the earliest can't be home until November, oh I wish I could
have you out here with me. Thats the punishment I get for being
too good at my ground subjects — strange isn't it. Anyway when I
finish that course & O.T.U. I'll be on coastal command & I really
prefer that work. None of the boys are to be instructors which suprised
me quite a bit — guess they don't need anymore now.
        One of my friends who is going home may go to
my home & maybe to yours if he gets the chance — he comes from
Bromley, Kent & does a lot of cycling — he is a nice fellow who
has worked very hard to get through, especially as he had only
an elementary education — he speaks proper London ~~...~~ is big
hearted, I hope he'el be able to come round — his name is Doug.
Wiltshire. I'm just going up to the mail now darling & then to dinner,
I'll be with you soon.
        Here I am again, there wasn't any mail & the dinner
was pretty bad as usual. Well darling I don't know quite what to
write about now as I am pretty blue — I love you an awful lot
& pray that you will wait for me, I'll try hard to get home as soon
as I can, you can do as you like about your holiday, I may get
home this year & yet things are so uncertain I can't really say.

10ᵗʰ August 1944

Hullo my darling Boo,

Again I must apologise for neglecting you a couple of days but honestly my darling I have been so terribly occupied rushing around the camp trying to get everything fixed up. To-morrow is our big day — on Tuesday we had our graduation dance & last night our dinner & party — phew what a night, some of us had to get up at 9.0 a.m. this morning to go & clean up down there — what a mess it was & many to the headache this morning. The dinner was excellent — half a spring chicken & many other tasty things — there were about 8 speeches & all were pretty good, the Group Capt: paid us & English in general great compliments he said that our course average was one of the highest on record & that considering that Dauphin is the toughest school in Canada to get through we must be pretty good pilots — I believe he meant it too, he is a very nice man & the boys all think he's just the tops — he was a pilot in the R.F.C. in England in the last war & is a great admirer of Englishmen.

Well my beautiful I have all my leave arranged & we are managing to get off earlier than the 18ᵗʰ. Officially us G.R. boys have to stay here a week after to graduation but we have managed to arrange it so that we leave on Tuesday night 15ᵗʰ Aug. Tomorrow we are going on a 48 to Winnipeg & so will be able to go with the lads who are going home via Moncton. As it stands we have our births booked on the train across Canada — those with commissions getting 1ˢᵗ class berths (I hope I'm one of them) — we are having a day in Montreal & then its only a 12 hr. run to New York, we should get there in about 4 days from here.

Everybody is sewing stripes on ek. all getting ready for to-morrow — those who get commissions take down their stripes & wear a big white armlet on their left arm until they can get a uniform. Most of the boys are packed — gee I wished I were going home too. Oh well after all I'm realizing an old ambition of mine, that is to stay in New York. You'll have to excuse the writing & this whole letter as its the morning after the night before —— I wasn't in a bad way but you should have seen some of them. They were wearing the instructors hats & then filling them with beer — beer was everywhere, one link instructor was running around in his pants, oh it was mad! To crown everything at 1.0 a.m. there was a terrific storm & roofs were blown off — however hardly any fellows knew there was a storm until we told them this morning. The S.P.'s were sent to keep order & they went home tight themselves — boy what fun.

Chapter 11

Graduation

A new Graduation Day was fixed and preparations for the 'bull parade' were made. All those to receive their wings would receive them as sergeants even though a number would be told before the parade that they would be commissioned as officers. The RCAF commissioned most of their pilots but the RAF were not so generous – although on an RCAF station Dad says they still came under the RAF. The commissioning of most of the Canadian lads on Dad's course was not liked by the RAF boys as in many cases the Canadians had not done as well as their counterparts who would end up without commissions.

Prior to the parade all were issued with sergeant's stripes and warned by the SWO that these must be sewn onto their tunics even if they knew they were being commissioned – he threatened that any found only to have pinned their strips on for the parade would lose their commission. Dad got his dancing partner to sew his stripes to his uniform for him.

Again I say it is worth reading the extract of letters as these give a picture of the build-up to the Wings Parade, and show the importance of the groundwork examinations and how the boys whilst treating them seriously were still able to have a laugh and place bets on who would come out top. It seems from the letter that Dad was 6 to 1 to win and finally came fifth – his backers did their best for him making sure he had plenty of sleep!

Graduation Day is a big occasion and treated as such by the RCAF, not only for those who were to receive their Wings, but for their mums and dads, sisters and brothers, and for the rest of the station who were to parade, support and witness the ceremony. The great day arrived – and so did the rain! It was August and should have been baking hot. Those responsible for organising had to quickly move proceedings to a hanger

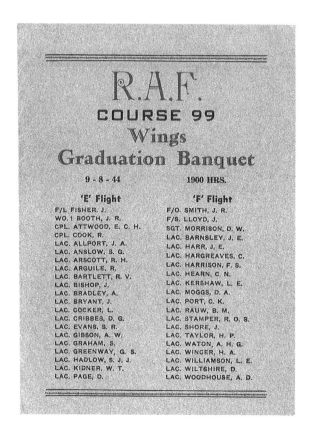

R.A.F.

COURSE 99
Wings
Graduation Banquet

9 - 8 - 44   1900 HRS.

'E' Flight	'F' Flight
F/L FISHER, J.	F/O. SMITH, J. R.
WO. 1 BOOTH, J. R.	F/S. LLOYD, J.
CPL. ATTWOOD, E. C. H.	SGT. MORRISON, D. W.
CPL. COOK, R.	LAC. BARNSLEY, J. E.
LAC. ALLPORT, J. A.	LAC. HARR, J. E.
LAC. ANSLOW, S. G.	LAC. HARGREAVES, C.
LAC. ARSCOTT, R. H.	LAC. HARRISON, F. S.
LAC. ARGUILE, R.	LAC. HEARN, C. N.
LAC. BARTLETT, R. V.	LAC. KERSHAW, L. E.
LAC. BISHOP, J.	LAC. MOGGS, D. A.
LAC. BRADLEY, A.	LAC. PORT, C. K.
LAC. BRYANT, J.	LAC. RAUW, B. M.
LAC. COCKER, L.	LAC. STAMPER, R. O. S.
LAC. CRIBBES, D. G.	LAC. SHORE, J.
LAC. EVANS, S. R.	LAC. TAYLOR, H. P.
LAC. GIBSON, A. W.	LAC. WATON, A. H. G.
LAC. GRAHAM, S.	LAC. WINGER, H. A.
LAC. GREENWAY, G. S.	LAC. WILLIAMSON, L. E.
LAC. HADLOW, S. J. J.	LAC. WILTSHIRE, D.
LAC. KIDNER, W. T.	LAC. WOODHOUSE, A. D.
LAC. PAGE, D.	

and the parade was duly formed up with tiers of seats being arranged inside for the visitors – not great numbers however, since this was largely an RAF course to be honoured and there would be no parents from the UK. There were of course one or two WDs and local girlfriends who took the place of the RAF boys' mums and dads! The two flights of the course were drawn up outside the hanger and the stripes inspected, and at the appropriate signal they marched in to the strains of music provided by the station band.

On parade the procedure, after the preliminaries of introduction by the station commander, was for each man to march forward when his name was called, halt in front of the presentation stand, salute, have the 'Wings Brevet' pinned to his chest, salute, about turn and march back to his position in his flight. When a man's name was called it was followed by where

The London boys immediately after graduation.

he came from, and Dad had previously sensed that largely, because of the Blitz and the many months of bombing that London had suffered, those coming from there were held in special regard by Canadians and indeed Americans alike. Thus Dad said he was not surprised that when a man's name was called followed by 'of London' there was a murmur from the audience – and when about one in five of the RAF boys came from London the murmur gradually increased as more London boys went forward to receive their wings. Dad has a photograph of the London boys taken after the parade and there was a demand by some who lived as far out as Reading and Brighton to get into the act. It is quite strange when you look back on it, but at the time it did not seem at all unusual to want people to think you came from London, anymore than you were proud to be British.

After the parade and the applause was over, twelve men, all the Canadians on the course, Dad seems to remember, and the other boys from the RAF were summoned to the Commanding Officer and told they had been awarded commissions – Dad was one of the lucky few. It seems from the letters that he had previously been advised that he was not going home but was to take a further course on Prince Edward Island, a GR course (General Reconnaissance). This was a course designed to get pilots more

ROYAL CANADIAN AIR FORCE

OUR FILE
REF. YOUR
DATED

Dauphin, Manitoba.
10th August, 1944.

PERSONAL

GB180A757 P/O B.A. Moggs,
No. 10 S.F.T.S., RCAF.,
Dauphin, Manitoba.

Dear Pilot Officer Moggs:

Please accept my sincere congratulations on your appointment as a Pilot Officer.

You have been selected to hold the King's Commission because of the good results you have obtained in your training and because your officers and instructors consider that you possess the qualifications and abilities that are required in a leader.

The standards of the commissioned officers in the Royal Canadian Air Force are high, and I am depending on you to measure up to them.

The service expects you to provide not only leadership in your work but also to set an example, both on and off duty, in discipline, in department, in appearance and in all your personal behaviour.

All junior ranks will look to you for leadership and you must at all times realize your obligations and duty to maintain and set high standards by which they will be governed.

I wish you the best of success in the assumption of your new duties and responsibilities, and I know that you will live up to all the fine traditions of the Royal Canadian Air Force.

Yours very truly,

(.C. Huggard) G/C
C.O., No. 10 S.F.T.S., RCAF.,
Dauphin, Manitoba.

R.C.A.F. G. 32
2000M-5-43 (3277)
H.Q. 885-G-32

deeply involved in Navigation for particular use with Coastal Command. On hearing his posting he had at first tried to get it changed but was advised by the Flight Commander not to try – this is reported in one of Dad's letters.

The Graduation Dinner took place two nights before the Wings Parade on the 9 August 1944 – most of those Dad had dinner with that night he would never see again and it was sad, he said, to lose so many friends he had made both on that course and earlier. Dad's letter of 10th August is worth reading to see some of the high jinks they got up to at that dinner.

Dad said that all the anger and disappointments over delays in the courses had been forgotten and those lucky enough to have survived Course 99 were now, albeit temporarily, happier than they had ever been.

Chapter 12

Now you are a Pilot on Leave in New York!

Those of Course 99 due to report to GR School were all commissioned officers, two from Dad's flight (only three RAF boys from that flight had been commissioned), and initially they were told they would have to stay at Dauphin a further week and then report to PEI early in September.

They were told to go to Winnipeg to get their uniforms – officers were given an allowance and bought their own uniforms – and they joined the lads going home on their train to Winnipeg where after one final night out they said farewell. Dad and his GR colleagues were measured up for uniforms at, Dad seems to remember, The Hudson Bay Company department store – the uniforms to be ready in a matter of two or three days.

Dad says that since he was in Winnipeg he thought he ought to go and see the people who had been so kind to him the previous Christmas, and so he visited Stonewall – he says he has no idea how he got there as he cannot remember catching a bus (it was about 25 miles outside Winnipeg) but feels he must have done. Anyway he stayed with his friends overnight and they tried to get him to stay with them for his leave instead of going to New York – Dad says he found it difficult to say no but he so wanted to go to New York that he declined their offer, and the next day Mr Hutson drove him to Winnipeg station to catch his train back to Dauphin. As I have said earlier, Dad did see Mr Hutson again when he was able to entertain him and his new wife at his home in England some twelve years later – he never saw Mrs Hutson again as this dear lady died soon after the War. Dad really regretted this as she had been so nice to him and his friends when they stayed there Christmas 1943.

17ª August 1944.

My dear Bette,

I have several apologies to make to you for not having written for a few days but actually dear I have been going about almost in a dream — things have been pretty hectic & I haven't had anytime to spare. I hope you'll believe me when I say I'm deeply sorry for having left you waiting so long for a letter. At the moment I am on the Canadian National Continental Express somewhere north of Lake Superior travelling East to Montreal — we have been travelling for about 15 hours so far & we arrive to-morrow mornings. That is 15 hrs. from Winnipeg, we arrived in that city yesterday morning & left last night. We are off to New York for 14 days leave — I hope you received my cablegram O.K. & that you understood it. I graduated on Friday & received my commission — there were only 12 commissions on the course & only 3 of them were in my flight. Paddy Morrison, Alan Vivier & myself — so now I am a P/O & have my uniform & everything (please excuse this writing but this train is rocking quite a bit). I must admit I feel very pleased with myself, this uniform kind of suits me & so does this officers life. Boy, I'm pleased I made it — Thankyou darling I owe it all to you. — it is through you that I have worked so hard to get through — I remembered you saying that friends of yours had officers for boyfriends so I figured well if they can then why shouldn't my Bette have an officer, so here I am. I'll get a photograph taken as soon as I get an opportunity & send it to you. I'm hoping, being a very conceited person, that you'll be proud of me now — I only wished I could have been coming home but as it is I am going to the G.R. course on P.E.I. There are 7 of us going to G.R & we all have commissions & we are all going to New York for leave having to report to P.E.I. on the 2nd Sept. I'm very excited & looking forward to it tremendously.

I'll try & tell you what has happened since graduation — the parade was at 4·0 p.m. on Friday 11th & according to everybody it was a very smart parade indeed, I was very nervous when it was my turn to go forward — Sgt. Maggs, London, England — however I did everything correctly. After the parade 12 of us were called out to go to see the C.O. — it was to tell us we had been granted commission — he gave a white band for our arms & a letter confirming our commission. Then we all went & had refreshments with the visitors, of whom there were quite a number — after that those of us who were officers were invited by the C.O. to the Mess. Gosh they treated us well — free drinks & everybody coming and introducing himself. Later that night we managed to get away from the mess to catch the train for Winnipeg with the rest of the boys who are on their way home. We only had a 4½ & I took opportunity of this by going to visit Stonewall where I stayed

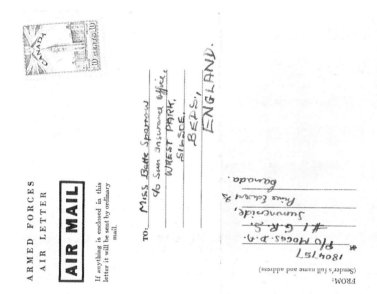

at Xmas — after first of all fixing up our uniform in Winnipeg. Mr & Mrs Hutson were very pleased to see me & tried to make me spend part of this leave with them — but having fixed everything on the train etc. I didn't accept, in any case they could hardly expect me to forego a chance of seeing New York. I was kept quite busy there & on Sunday evening Mr Hutson drove me to Winnipeg so as I could catch my train. On Monday we were busy all day getting clearance from the station & in the evening again went to the mess — incidently we were eating our meals in the mess & the food & the fact of being waited on gave me quite an apetite for a change. Tuesday we left for Winnipeg & arrived Wednesday morning — I picked up my uniform & put it on immediately — it fits very well indeed — last evening we caught this train in which we have 1st class sleeping berths with 1$ & 1.25$ tickets for meals — it's a great life. We have nearly a day in Montreal & then we go down to New York which is a 12 hr. run.

Back to Dauphin and the final farewells to instructors and, as Dad said, the 'girls' from the WDs. One particular friend of Dad, who he had had as a partner in his dancing class, lent him her camera to take to New York knowing that he could only return it by post – she must have been a good friend, Dad, I said!

Then it was off to New York by train, first to Winnipeg to collect the uniforms and then on the Transcontinental to Montreal which took about two days. Dad wrote a letter whilst on the train and this can be seen by the reader (see 17 August 1944).

There were big gaps in Dad's memory but he certainly retained some good recollections of his time in New York – it was, he said, one of the highlights of his life; so how could he forget.

It seems they arrived in Montreal from Winnipeg in the morning and, after spending the day there, took a night train down to New York but, since they had to pay for this part of the journey, they elected to sit up in a night coach rather than paying for sleepers.

Dad recalls the thrill of arriving in New York early the next morning, and they at once set about finding the English Speaking Union Officers' Club to which they had been advised to go from previous RAF visitors to the city.

Having breakfasted they duly arrived by taxi at the address of the Union and were soon being 'registered' and being asked their requirements for their stay. The English Speaking Union was to become their base and Dad could not say enough in praise of the hospitality and friendship offered them by this friendly institution. It was an unusual place with tea being served in the afternoon by a lady with a large brimmed hat. On entering you were asked to take tea with this lady and then passed on to the numerous hostesses, many of whom had obviously been recruited from the more wealthy families in New York, mostly Americans, but sprinkled with a few English who were lucky enough to be able to spend the War in the States.

It was a good spot to meet and relax and of course it was there that your stay in New York was arranged. Not all the lads with my father wanted the same type of accommodation. On offer was staying with a family in New York, staying with a family on Long Island – this they were told would include sailing, fishing etc., or having an apartment in New York on their own and not to be tied to a family. Dad and one of his friends opted for the latter since both wanted to see New York on their own and not to be tied to a family.

It was August and very hot, so the apartments on offer were from families who had gone north, to Maine or somewhere cooler, to get away from the heat of the city. Derek Cribbes, who Dad remembers spoke English with a public school accent, was in fact an Argentinian of British stock who had only been to England when he joined the RAF. He came from Buenos Aires and was good company, liking the same things as Dad – what was that? Well, as far as I can tell, it was a good time, shows, parties, sightseeing, nightclubs and girls!

Having made their choice soon after their arrival at the club, Derek and Dad were directed to an apartment off Madison Avenue in one of the streets in the eighties, Dad couldn't remember which one, but thought it was 81st St. It appeared that this apartment had been put forward as for one person only but the lady at the Union reckoned they could manage two as she said the apartments were quite big and there would only be a housekeeper resident.

Dad said they pressed the bell at the front door which was on the street, and shortly afterwards were greeted by a middle-aged lady who, when they said who had sent them, expressed surprise that two had been sent. Dad remembered well what she had said, 'My goodness they have sent two of you and there's only one bathroom.' Dad said we assured her we would manage somehow, and when they were shown the bathroom he said they were both agreed they would happily have bedded down in there – it was like nothing Dad had seen before. They had been told the owners were shipping millionaires and would not be back until after the summer. Each was given a key to the flat and advised that there would be no food – that they would have to provide for themselves. Dad says that was the last time they saw the lady and yet at whatever time they returned after a day or night out they always found their beds made and the bathroom clean.

New York in 1944 was another world – all the lights ablaze, shops open all hours, restaurants, nightclubs, theatres, cinemas, everything was as if there were no war and in deep contrast to London with its blackout and general war atmosphere. There were of course men in uniform, but not nearly so many as in London when Dad had last been there when every other person seemed to be in the services.

In the first day or two in New York Dad said he hardly got to bed; in the day there were the sights to see and in the evening there was a theatre, cinema or nightclub and plenty of bars. It was difficult to spend money as so many people wanted to buy drinks when they learnt you were RAF pilots – it was great. Dad recalls going to a film on Broadway which featured the RAF and on coming out of the cinema Dad and his friends were practically mobbed by well-wishers. Dad tells me they were brought a bit down to earth shortly after this when, in a bar near the cinema, one man asked them if they were in the fire service – he obviously hadn't seen the film!

Up the Empire State and the Rockefeller Center, down to the Battery, up to Harlem, and then Greenwich Village. The visit to the latter was one of Dad's highlights; they took a cab to go down town when Dad said Derek started to talk to the cab driver in Spanish. Derek had spotted the driver's identity card which showed a Spanish name – the man replied in Spanish and the long and short of it was that he took them to a very special club in the Village which had a floor show with a Spanish flavour, Flamenco dancers, etc., and a terrific menu.

There were plenty of girls at the English Speaking Union and they were allowed to date – both Derek and Dad went out with girls from the club. Dad says he went out with a John Powers girl – a beautiful blonde who came from Brooklyn and talked like it. Powers girls, who were models, were well-known at the time for their beauty and had become known, even back home, through a picture, he believed – *Powers Girls* with Rita Hayworth or someone similar in the starring role.

He also met the daughter of a wealthy English gentleman, and spent a couple of evenings with them. Then there was the girl from Queens, a

Leave in New York.

New York 'High Society' – a garden party.

long ride out on the Jamaica line – all at the price of a nickle. The subways were very good for getting about and Dad says he became very familiar with them. Most of the stations had four tracks through them and thus there were expresses which would get you out to the deep suburbs in no time, unlike the London tube which is forced to stop at every station when underground.

Then there was the relative Dad had in New Jersey whom he had met briefly when a boy when this man and his family visited England in the early thirties. Dad had written to Uncle John (he was actually my grandfather's cousin) whilst in Canada and resolved to see him if it were not too far from New York. Derek was very self-sufficient and did not want to leave New York, so Dad took a train to Ocean Grove to find his relative. It turned out to be a visit he quite enjoyed but was a little too restrictive for him at the time. His relatives were quite hospitable but were very religious and didn't approve of Dad going to Asbury Park, the adjoining town, and taking a girl to a nightclub and being photographed with her. He remembered particularly the church to which he was taken and witnessing the collection of baskets full of paper money. Ocean Grove was a religious community with gates to roads entering town and no cars were allowed on the roads on Sundays. There was a nice beach but nothing else, but the adjoining Asbury Park had more to offer.

In later years Dad returned the hospitality on two occasions when his relative visited Britain again.

Dad was not sorry to get back to New York where he felt free, although everyone had been kind to him in New Jersey.

Dad seems to have packed a lot into this stay in New York including two visits to radio broadcasts, one to see Alan Jones (a well-known film-star singer) and an orchestra supposed to be playing on Stradivarius; the other where members of the audience related interesting happenings: one old lady in a strong New York accent related how her mother was in the audience of the Ford Theatre in Washington when Abraham Lincoln had been assassinated.

The big show in New York was *Oklahoma*, and the general public had great difficulty in getting tickets. However, every week there was a special performance for service personnel in uniform and Dad was thus able to get a ticket – he still has the program and said he had never seen anything like it. It seems the music, which was on all the jukeboxes in North America, was not allowed to be played in the UK until the show itself reached London a couple of years after the War had ended.

The list of events and memories of this short break in New York shows just how much New York had been impressed on Dad's mind, but all good things come to an end and there was a war on, although one would never have known it if one had been there at that time.

Thus it was back to the real world leaving the big city to carry on as if nothing in the world outside affected it in any way.

It was now up to Montreal and then on to Summerside, a journey of over a 1,000 miles. Dad has no recollection of that particular journey which probably took two days; they slept on the trains.

G R School and Montreal

Summerside was a small town with an RCAF station for training navigators. The sea crossing was quite short and part of the train was carried on the ferry. The planes used on the station were Anson 5s with which Dad was to become very familiar, but not just then. No, having duly arrived at the station on time the boys were told to take another two weeks leave as they were not ready for them. Well it was frustrating but Dad said they all thought they could manage another two weeks in New York. Money was no problem as they had not spent too much on their leave and getting RCAF officers' pay was a tremendous boost to their income, they would still have enough for another leave. They took the necessary steps to make the long journey back but were thwarted as they were informed that the border had now been closed due to a polio scare. There was nothing for it but to spend the leave in Canada and the only place worth visiting in Eastern Canada was Montreal, 700 miles from PEI.

Dad cannot remember much of his stay in Montreal. They certainly had no free accommodation, but he did remember a girl he met who worked in a big department store. All stores' employees were bi-lingual and the majority were of French extraction. He also vaguely remembers going to a football match at the McGill University, but with most in Montreal his mind was quite blank; it obviously did not impress. He says he remembers crowds at the railway station one day and was told that the former mayor of the city had just been released from internment. Apparently he had been a staunch supporter of Vichy France – whether what Dad was told was correct he did not know but certainly had the impression that the French people in Montreal were not exactly friendly.

The girl he met with whom he spent part of his leave showed him a few places of interest including Mount Royal after which the city is named. He said he has no wish to return there.

Chapter 13

GR on Prince Edward Island

Back in Summerside the course started in earnest – plenty of ground work and then flying on the long trips over the Gulf of St Lawrence up to the Gaspé Peninsular, a spot then noted for birds nesting on the cliffs. Flying was at low altitudes over the sea both day and night, sometimes as First Navigator and sometimes as Second Navigator. Flying low below cloud was usually very bumpy, and Dad said he hated it as First Navigator when bumpy as it made him airsick; the trips lasted three to four hours. As First Navigator, one sat on one's parachute at a small desk with a chart and a small instrument called a computor (but nothing to do with the machines used today and called computers) whilst working out the course for the pilot to fly. All navigating was on dead reckoning and there were only a few fixes to check your position whilst over the sea, and of course checking the wind speed and direction was of vital importance in fixing the course. There were none of the guides used today when flying. At night one checked wind speed by opening the door of the aircraft and dropping flares into the sea from which the drift could be measured. Night flying was much less bumpy than day flying which was invariably below low cloud. Apart from the training aspect, these planes were used for observing shipping and reporting submarines which might be lurking to pounce on shipping leaving the St Lawrence or moving up the coast from St John or Halifax to the St Lawrence.

The training at Summerside was intensive and there was little spare time. Although some of the lads went to the island's capital, Charlottetown, Dad says he doesn't remember going, and feels he must have missed a trip there. He reminded me that PEI was where the famous story, *Anne of Green Gables*, was located. The island is quite big and very rural. Most people Dad spoke to had never left the island to visit the

139

Summerside, P.E.I. 1944.

mainland – mind you, Dad says, the mainland near to Prince Edward Island was probably more remote than the island itself, the nearest big city being many miles to the south. They often flew south to St John, New Brunswick, to photograph shipping in the harbour as part of their training, but even that city was no bigger than a small provincial town in England and not much bigger than Charlottetown on the island. The people in Summerside seemed to keep themselves to themselves and had little to do with the airforce personnel.

After nine weeks hard slog the course came to an end and Dad with some of the others received Navigators Certificates in the Royal Canadian Air Force. They also received their postings. Dad was destined for the Bahamas to fly Mitchells with conversion on to Liberators which were coming more into service in Coastal Command. Most of the lads posted to Nassau, Bahamas, were tickled pink with the thought of such a place. They looked upon it almost as if they were going on holiday – not so Dad! He had been away from home for over eighteen months and was getting worried that his fiancée might be finding friendship with too many Americans and other service personnel. As I said earlier, Betty was evacuated to a country mansion, which happened to be surrounded now by both American and RAF stations.

From what Dad had told me about young ladies he met whilst in Canada he of course had not been exactly true, and it was not difficult to imagine that his wife-to-be, in a similar situation, had been that much different. Who could blame them anyway? However, it was obvious that in spite of all the women he had known since last at home, he still wanted to marry Betty. So what did Dad do but try to get out of his posting and join those going back home. There was no shortage of volunteers to change; few wanted to go home and, as they all said, 'Be on ops in a matter of weeks.' The early clamour to get on ops of a year or so ago had long since been knocked out of these young men. Love does strange things and Dad could not be put off, so he pressed his case and was finally granted permission to swap – he did so with a married man who said he wasn't so keen to go home! Dad remembers his name well but would not let me know in case it could, even after all these years, embarrass someone.

There was a farewell party in the mess and then they hired a kite to take them to the mainland and some more leave – the plane was a Boeing and at the time for take-off there was thick fog on the ground and the pilot a civilian, was not anxious to take off. However, the lads were determined to go in order to make the train connection to get on the mainland, and they made it very difficult for the poor man to refuse to fly them – no fear at that age I suppose. Anyway flying at zero feet they left Summerside and landed safely on the mainland – Dad doesn't remember where or from where they caught the train taking them west to Montreal from whence they would again go south to New York!

Chapter 14

New York Again (What More Leave!)

Yes it was yet more leave before reporting back to Moncton, New Brunswick. Of course after their last leave there could be no other choice but New York.

Dad's particular friend on this trip was a young man he had met up with again at Summerside after not seeing him since they were separated by different postings over a year earlier. Fred had not been on leave in New York before but instead had spent an earlier leave in Louisville, Kentucky. Pre-war he had had a pen friend at school who lived in that city and hence the visit – his stories of his trip to Louisville, Dad said, were out of this world. He must have been the only Englishman to visit there during that part of the War and, as he had come from London, they had eaten up his stories of the London Blitz and printed them on the front page of dailies (he produced these as evidence of the truth of his story) – and the girls . . . Dad said they all thought of getting Fred to take them to Louisville. Anyway, New York it was and Dad and Fred duly went along to the English Speaking Union Officers' Club to get fixed up for their leave. Derek, who had shared accommodation previously when in New York, was not able to accompany them.

At the Club Dad asked about the previous accommodation he had had in the city but was told that as it was November the owners were now back in town. Of the type of place Dad and Fred wanted there was only one in New York available – 'You get a room and breakfast too,' they were told. 'Now the place you are going to belongs to Mrs Roosevelt.' Dad said the expected surprise worked and straightaway the lady sorting out the accommodation laughed and said, 'No, it's not the President's wife. This lady is a niece of Theodore Roosevelt – and if you go there please don't speak too much about FDR as he is the blacksheep of the family, he being

142

UNITED NATIONS OFFICERS' CLUB
21 EAST 54TH STREET
NEW YORK 22, N. Y.
Plaza 8-1815

Introducing _P/O MOGGS & P/O GREEN_

To _MRS Philip J. Roosevelt_
31 East 72d Street

On _____ At _____

RH 4-1433

I'm so sorry not to
see you to say
good-bye — and sorry
I haven't seen more
of you while you were
here. I do hope
you've had a good
time in New York &
that you'll get safely
& quickly on to your
next place — all good
luck to the marriage —
Jean D. Roosevelt

2nd leave in new York.

a Democrat and the family being Republican as of course was Theodore when he was President.'

Having got over the shock the two young men made their way to the apartment which was somewhere on one of the streets off Park Avenue, near Madison.

A lift to the floor (Dad doesn't remember which one) opened straight into the apartment and they were met by the maid who showed them where their room was located. They must have been given a key and they were told that they would have breakfast with Mrs Roosevelt.

The New York leave was as good as the first and Mrs Roosevelt was a lovely and kind lady – Dad still holds the note she left for him when he left to return to the station. Dad remembers a Thanksgiving dinner with a family in New York, a visit and dinner at the Waldorf Astoria with a young lady, and being interviewed on television in the Rockefeller Center. The latter came about when being conducted around the Center – it seems a lady taking an interest in the four or five RAF officers walking around came up to them and said she wanted to interview one of them, and without letting them recover their breath got hold of Dad's arm and said, 'You will volunteer won't you!'

Dad was taken to a studio in the building whilst the others in the party were left to look at the television screen sited near to where they had been walking. Dad says he doesn't remember much of the interview which centred on where he came from, and how did New York compare with London. On his return to his friends he says his leg was pulled something terrible as some ladies in the 'audience' were heard to say, 'Oh isn't he nice.' Dad says the TV was probably a closed circuit throughout the Center. TV was then quite in its infancy, although he remembers a television set being in the apartment where he stayed when he first visited New York – they never saw it working.

The dinner in the Waldorf was, he seems to remember, in The Diamond Horseshoe which had been featured in a Hollywood film with, he believes, Betty Grable as the star.

His friend, Fred, had to be shown the usual sights, Radio City Music Hall, The Empire State, Wall Street, Greenwich Village, etc., but he had to leave before Dad as his posting to Nassau was due. Dad a couple of days later made his own way back to Moncton. It was November and, having left New York on a cold day, the train going north to Montreal soon was passing through snow, light at first but the further north they went so the snow became heavier and the train slowed. Dad had to catch a connection at Montreal and if he missed it would have to wait a day for the next one. The train stopped at various stations getting later and later, and the snow got thicker and thicker. The conductor, knowing Dad's problem, came up with the idea of Dad leaving the train at Lachine Junction and getting the Transcontinental Express from there. The only snag was the Transcontinental was not due to stop at Lachine and he would have to get through to Montreal to see if it could be arranged. He obviously succeeded for Dad and, after duly thanking the conductor, was unloaded at Lachine and after waiting about half an hour the mighty Transcontinental steamed into the station and slowed to a stop. The train with perhaps sixteen coaches looked tremendous, and the engine hauling the train dwarfed Dad as he stood below; there was no platform. The conductor of the train soon opened a door and Dad was helped on board and taken to his sleeping berth which he had booked in New York. Dad is not sure what time it was but seems to remember it was the early hours of the morning. He was of course the only person to board the train at that station and being brought up in a railway family, his dad, grandfather and uncle were all drivers on the LNER, he could hardly get over the fact that the mighty Transcontinental had stopped just for him – his dad would think it inconceivable – but it happened.

Chapter 15

Moncton and Home

He duly arrived in Moncton and then began the wait – the wait for the ship to take him back to England. How many weeks he would be there he had no idea. It was a few weeks before Christmas 1944.

Moncton was a small town with not too many shops but he had to get some presents to take home – he managed to get something small for his family and bought, what he thought was a fabulous ski-coat for his wife-to-be. He told me afterwards that his wife did in fact like the coat very much for it was far superior to anything then available in England even if one had the spare ration coupons – she wore the coat for many years (not all the time of course!) and it was finally destroyed, Dad said, in 1967 when she used it to put out a frying pan fire in their home – she had been using it in later years as something warm to put on when putting the washing out in cold weather.

Moncton provided, in its small way, some entertainment – dancing at a small hall, a cinema on camp, one or two restaurants. Dad said he had his fill of steaks, the last he would get for goodness knows how long, whilst in Moncton – including some at the apartment of a young lady he met there.

Eventually the day to leave arrived and, now joined with another group of aircrew, he boarded a train heavily loaded with kit bound for Halifax, Nova Scotia, where their ship was waiting. Dad remembers struggling along the quay with his kit, for even though an officer he was responsible for looking after it himself.

The ship was the new *Mauretania*, big but not anywhere near the size of the *Queen Mary* on which he had crossed a year and a half earlier. Dad said it seemed strange going home; it was as if he had been in a dream and now he was waking up – a dream maybe, but what a dream – and what

Moncton, New Brunswick.

memories. People would be bored by hearing them for years, he said. But how could you blame him; it was such an experience. His last act in Moncton had been to return the camera to the WD in Dauphin who, knowing she was never likely to see him again, had entrusted him to return it to her. She had also given him a present for his marriage but he never saw her again. She would be in her eighties now, Dad added.

On board ship and duly allocated to sleeping accommodation they were all advised by more senior officers what was required of them during the voyage. Unlike the voyage over as an LAC he was now a Pilot Officer and thus the personal scrubbing of decks was not the likely task. Precisely what Dad did he was not very clear. He said he seemed to remember he was officer in charge of anti-aircraft but cannot reconcile this with his training. He cannot remember any guns but knows there must have been some, and as for knowledge of how to fire them he said they would have to have been Browning machine guns as that was the only gun with which he was familiar. In later years, when thinking back, he thinks he might have been responsible, for airmen used to keep watch for aircraft – all he can remember is a picture of visiting men on deck, fed up to the teeth with their turn on watch, and speaking to one or two of them. The rest of the voyage is blank, except he remembers that before they sailed the Captain announced over the Tannoy that he would do his best to get them back in England for Christmas – it was then, Dad says, the 17th December.

The *Mauretania* crossed the Atlantic unescorted but she had not the speed of the 'Mary' – although built after the 'Mary' she had not been built to compete on the very fast crossings of the *Normandie, Queen Mary, Queen Elizabeth, Rex*, etc. – her speed was good but typically twenty-two knots against thirty plus of the Blue Riband liners. Dad says that some years after the War he had an argument over the speed of the *Mauretania*. His friend at work who had been a minesweeper captain in the War had said the *Mauretania* had been built to capture the Blue Riband. Dad says he knew the man was wrong and proved it by telephoning Cunard to settle the argument. How Dad was so certain was that he remembered very well the comments made by those who had been on Coastal Command courses where they had been told how with snorkel German submarines could travel below water at up to twenty knots – which as the lads said was practically the speed of the *Mauretania* travelling unescorted.

They obviously had an uneventful voyage and a week later were told they had arrived at the mouth of the Mersey, but were told they would not be able to dock until the next day as there was thick fog . . . Christmas Day! Christmas Dinner had been served on Christmas Eve, it being fully expected that the ship would dock later that day. The dinner had been enjoyed but now gloom fell over the ship – fancy docking on Christmas Day!

Christmas Day arrived and the fog cleared sufficiently for the docking to take place, but almost immediately the dockside was empty and the passengers were informed that they would not be able to disembark until Boxing Day. Whether the cookhouse crew had managed to get off the ship, and who could blame them if they had, he did not know but he knows that for Christmas Day meals they were issued with American K Rations which were small packets of food for use when there were no catering facilities.

Dad could not remember whether they even got off the next day as when they did they were entrained for Harrogate but seems to remember they had to change trains at York and whilst waiting for the connection he telephoned his fiancée. There was no telephone at her home and thus she must have been at work which almost certainly meant it was not Boxing Day. He said he remembers how strange her voice sounded after getting used to hearing Canadian and American women's voices for so long.

At Harrogate Dad was placed in the Queens Hotel which was the aircrew distribution centre for returning pilots and navigators. There were certain formalities to go through and disembarkation leave was awaited impatiently. On one of the notice boards Dad read 'All aircrew officers intending marrying whilst on leave should report to the station adjutant's

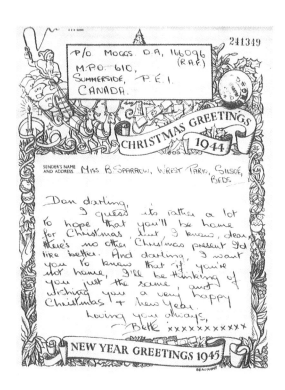

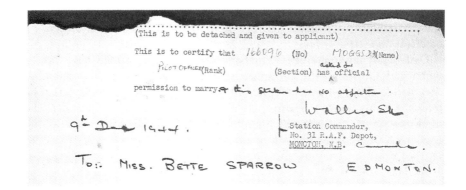

office.' Dad duly went along and showed the authorisation to marry he had obtained from the station Padre in Moncton. He advised of the details so that the appropriate pay arrangements could be made and then the adjutant started to talk about where Dad's next move would likely be. 'Of course you will most likely be posted to the Far East. By the way, are you insured?'

'No,' Dad replied, 'I thought insurance companies did not cover death or injury from war.'

'Ah but did you know,' continued the adjutant, 'that most of the deaths out east are from tropical diseases which are covered?' To cut a long story short the adjutant sold Dad an insurance policy – £20 per annum – quite a lot of money at that time when you consider that Dad's salary before he went in to the services was only £130 per annum.

The end of this particular story is worth telling now even though it came about a little later. It appears that the insurance company – Legal and General – sent the policy to where Dad's new wife was living and, there not being copying machines, she wrote out the whole thing in longhand and sent it to Dad. He still has the document. Dad duly received it and read it through one evening when he had nothing better to do. It clearly stated that death or injury caused through tropical diseases was not covered. Dad realised then that he had been tricked and on his next leave went to their main office in Lower Regent Street and confronted them with the story. They of course cancelled the policy but although he has, he said, often laughed about it since he was at the time very angry and he wondered how many others had been conned by this unscrupulous man who probably, Dad said, ended up chairman of the company.

After seeing the adjutant, Dad was able to advise his intended and family that he would be home on New Year's Day and arriving at King's Cross at such and such a time, and would arrive home an hour or so later. He hoped that Betty would meet him and when he got to the London terminus he found the whole family there; Mum and Dad looking proud of their Pilot Officer son and Betty somewhat embarrassed at having to face Dad with the whole family present. Grandad grabbed Dad's trunk and swinging it up on his shoulder managed to break the handle – the first of a series of things that were to go wrong on his leave.

The wedding had been arranged for January 3rd giving very little time to do anything in between, a fact that did not please his parents and he straightaway sensed some tension. Betty had managed to arrange for a honeymoon, a week in Colwyn Bay which she understood would probably be away from the barbed wire beaches and gun emplacements which covered much of the English coastline.

It was, Dad said, the time of the doodle-bugs or buzz bombs or rather it was the end of the time of them and the beginning of the V-2 rockets. Not much news except through letters which had filtered out of the country about these but London being the target had once again suffered badly and yet again young children had been evacuated to the country or at least away from London.

As Dad had sensed there was bad feeling over the wedding and his first evening at home was not at all pleasant. What it was all about Dad does not remember but guesses it was something to do with him getting married at such short notice – mind you he had been engaged over three years!

Dad remembered that it must have been whilst he was in Canada that he had learnt something about Grandad driving ambulance trains for the Americans. He thinks it was after he was back home that he learnt what it was all about. It seems that the American Army, with the agreement of railway companies in Britain, had advertised for railwaymen to drive their ambulance trains in Britain, and Grandad had been one of the scores who had applied for the jobs which would pay two or three times as much as the drivers were usually paid. Grandad was one of the few chosen for the work and was 'called to work for them' just prior to D-Day when he was required to report to Newbury which was to be the base for ambulance trains. Dad thinks that the depot was actually on the Newbury racecourse and he assumes there must therefore have been rail spurs built there. Grandad lived on the trains and he drove his trains to seaports, mostly Southampton, Dad thinks, and from there to various hospitals throughout the west and south of England. How long he was with them Dad didn't know but he said that his sister, Auntie Babs, went down there for one weekend and met many of the Americans attached to the train, all of whom were American Army personnel, including the doctors.

Chapter 16

The Wedding or The Rocket

The morning of the wedding arrived; Grandad was at work and Dad, after his breakfast, was in the scullery/kitchen polishing his shoes; his mother and sister were also there when it happened.

Dad says he has told this part of his life many times and it was obvious to me that his memory of the events were very clear. He told me that it was so vivid to him that it was clearer to him than things that had happened only a year or two ago. While cleaning his shoes Dad said he remembered the room suddenly dark and sparks appearing followed almost instantly by a tremendous noise and the screaming of his mother and sister – they had jumped to him clinging to him. They knew what had happened – seeing that his family were quite unharmed, Dad says, he rushed to the front of the house, the kitchen was at the back, to see what had happened. He ran through the opening where once the door had been and into the street. He was the only one out there. He ran along the street towards some screaming coming from a house opposite. He ran into the house following the crying up the stairs – someone was in the bathroom and crying out for her baby. The bathroom door was locked or jammed and hearing sobbing from an adjoining bedroom he rushed in and in the middle of a bed was a little girl crying. She was covered in ceiling plaster and her face was black with dirt except where her tears were falling, washing the dirt from her face. Dad says he grabbed the girl in his arms and went back to the bathroom. It was only then he realised the extent of the damage he had rushed into. There were sparks coming from electrical wiring. He called to the woman in the bathroom that her daughter was quite safe and that he would take the little girl outside and come back for her, but as he was going down the stairs two men entered the house and he hurriedly told them that the mother was in the bathroom and that when he had taken the young girl to his house across the road he would return to give a hand.

When he had first rushed into the street after the rocket had landed, there had been an eerie quietness, except for the crying from the house he had rushed into, but after getting the little girl back to his house things had suddenly come to life – there was now a great deal of activity and ambulances and wardens from adjoining streets had taken over. The lady in the bathroom had been taken out quickly by the men that had followed Dad into the house; she had been injured in one eye and unfortunately it was later learnt that she lost the sight of that eye. Only one person had been killed but the damage to property was extensive. It was of course a V-2 rocket which had fallen without warning – the crater was in the garden of the house opposite Dad's home. It was only when he returned to his home that he began to see the extent of the damage. The tiled roof of his parents' home had gone as too had the windows and door. In the front room, where he had left his uniform the night before, there was chaos. Plaster and lathe ceilings made such a mess – this was the room in which a few minutes before the blast they had had their breakfast. Now the remains of the breakfast and what was left of the table cloth were no longer there – they had been sucked out through the window – but the uniform was surprisingly still hanging on the picture rail. Well, that is, Dad said, you would never have known it was an RAF officer's uniform – it was white, white with plaster dust. But it was still there. The wedding was due to take place at All Saints Church in Edmonton about one and a half miles away. The question was, would he go through with the wedding?

Apart from the vivid memory of the blast and the immediate happenings Dad said he had since lost exactly what followed and how the decision to carry on was made. He remembers that one of the brothers of his wife-to-be came round on his bicycle to see where the rocket had fallen and to see if Dad was all right, and indeed whether the wedding was on or not. News always travelled fast as to where bombs had fallen particularly in daylight; first one saw the smoke, then heard the noise, and then began the speculation as to exactly where that one had landed. 'That looks as if it is over Bush Hill Park way', he could imagine Betty's family saying, and then someone volunteering to go over and see what had happened. How close it was to not happening and indeed for this story never to have been written is not worth thinking about – the crater was no more than twenty yards away from his home.

Dad says his best man was the next to arrive at his home – he had come from Enfield where the bush telegraph had told him that a rocket had

fallen near Bush Hill Park station. Dad reminded me that in those days very few people had telephones and so most of the information travelled by word of mouth. It appears that having decided to go ahead with the wedding Dad went with his uniform to his best man's house where a cleaning-up job was performed on it. I have seen the wedding photographs and from them it looks as if nothing had happened. Dad does not remember how they got to the wedding but guesses it must have been by bus from Enfield Town. Grandma and Grandad did not attend the wedding but Auntie Babs, Dad's sister, did. Three or four of his RAF colleagues who lived in London and were on leave made the effort and turned up for the wedding – Dad said the photographer said, 'Let me have one with your crew', which caused some amusement amongst them as they were all pilots.

The reception was held at a small hall in Winchmore Hall but Dad only remembers he and 'his crew' getting somewhat merry and singing 'Knock 'em in the Old Kent Road', a particular favourite of Dad's friend, Peter. The car duly arrived to take the couple to the Hotel Russell in London which Betty had booked and from whence they had been due to travel to Colwyn Bay the next day. The holiday was cancelled but they made the journey to town. They soon realised that it was not such a good idea to walk further into trouble. The whole night was filled with fire bells, explosions and the sound of ambulances tearing about. So different from New York, Dad said, where they hardly knew a war was on.

In later years Dad's wedding anniversary was never remembered as such by his mother. It was always, 'It's January 3rd today; this is the day of the rocket.'

Dad and his bride returned to Edmonton the following day and learnt that Betty's aunt had kindly given up her flat to them for the next week – her husband was overseas in the Army and she had arranged to stay at a friend's house. It was a wonderful unselfish gesture for which Dad says he was always grateful.

The week was spent helping his parents make something of their home; tarpaulin had been put on the roof and there were many jobs to be done. A young WAAF who lived a few doors from his parents had similarly been on leave when the bomb happened and she had come along to ask Dad, as an officer, to help her get an extension to her leave. Dad took the details, telephoned Air Ministry and arranged it for her. He did the same for himself and it was the latter which changed for him the whole outcome of his war – in fact he says in a way it helped him survive, although subsequent events hardly looked so auspicious at the time. These will unfold in the next chapter.

Chapter 17

Awaiting a Posting

The leave came to an end and it was off back to Harrogate to await his posting. He had only been away an extra seven days and was surprised to learn on return that all his latest group, that is, the ones he had returned with from Canada and those who had come to his wedding, had all been posted; he was on his own. He said he did not however, have long to wait for a posting and a few days later he was told to report to Hatfield. For Dad this seemed a good posting as he would be no more than an hour's bus ride from home, although of course his wife was still working in Bedfordshire and living most of the week there.

He was billeted in an old house between Hatfield and St Albans with several other aircrew, some of whom had been trained in Pensicola, USA, with the American Navy on Catalinas, a sturdy flying boat used extensively by RAF Coastal Command. Each morning the boys were taken by lorry to a relief drome the other side of Hatfield called Panshanger, which Dad learnt in later years had been the name of a country house where grand parties had been held in Victorian and Edwardian times. At Panshanger they flew Tiger Moths and got the impression they were being held there simply to keep occupied until a suitable posting arrived. After an initial check-out by an instructor, they were generally allowed to fly solo or with an instructor most anywhere they wanted within range.

Dad says he remembers how difficult it was to recognise the Panshanger field set amongst scores of other fields and without runways – it was so different from flying over the prairies. It was whilst at Panshanger that Dad made a flight to the country house where his wife was working. He made no preparations for the flight but on impulse decided when airborne. He had no difficulty in finding Luton and followed the road north towards Bedford and very soon saw the mansion, Wrest Park, set in the middle of a

Dear **Bert**

I am shortly proceeding overseas, and I am sending you the correct postal address which you should use *until you receive my open address* (see 3 below). This is:—

No. **166096** Rank **P/o** Name **MOGGS** Initials **D.R.**

HQ

Royal Air Force

c/o A.P.O. **8200**

2. The postage rate for ordinary letters will be 1½d. for the first ounce. Details of air-mail services available to the above address cannot be given, but Airgraphs (3d.) and air letters (3d. or 6d.) can be sent to most A.P.O. numbers, and such communications will be sent by air if possible. E.F.M. telegrams can be sent to certain A.P.O. numbers—details are obtainable from any Post Office.

3. On receipt of my open address full particulars of all postal and telegraph services can readily be obtained from any Post Office. These are generally:—
(i) Ordinary letters—1½d. 1st oz.; 1d. each additional oz.
(ii) Airgraphs 3d. (certain countries only)
(iii) Air letters 3d. or 6d. (most countries)
(iv) Air mail letters—Rates various (certain countries only)
(v) Ordinary, deferred or letter telegrams—Rates various.
(vi) E.F.M. telegrams 2½d. (British Empire and many destinations where Forces are serving.)

Remittances may be sent by postal order, except to Canada, Newfoundland and U.S.A. Limit £2 2s. 0d. per remitter per day.

4. For particulars regarding CSN telegrams (allowed for urgent and private business) which may be sent only by next-of-kin, enquire—For Officers—

Under Secretary of State,
Air Ministry,
Department AR 8, London.

For Airmen—
A.O. I/c The Record Office,
Royal Air Force,
Barnwood,
Gloucester.

Yours **with all my love**

Signature **Don**

M22227 12/44 JC&S 702

Dear **Mum & Dad**

I am shortly proceeding overseas, and I am sending you the correct postal address which you should use *until you receive my open address* (see 3 below). This is:—

No. **166096** Rank **P/o** Name **MOGGS** Initials **D.R.**

HQ

Royal Air Force

c/o A.P.O. **8200**

2. The postage rate for ordinary letters will be 1½d. for the first ounce. Details of air-mail services available to the above address cannot be given, but Airgraphs (3d.) and air letters (3d. or 6d.) can be sent to most A.P.O. numbers, and such communications will be sent by air if possible. E.F.M. telegrams can be sent to certain A.P.O. numbers—details are obtainable from any Post Office.

3. On receipt of my open address full particulars of all postal and telegraph services can readily be obtained from any Post Office. These are generally:—
(i) Ordinary letters—1½d. 1st oz.; 1d. each additional oz.
(ii) Airgraphs 3d. (certain countries only)
(iii) Air letters 3d. or 6d. (most countries)
(iv) Air mail letters—Rates various (certain countries only)
(v) Ordinary, deferred or letter telegrams—Rates various.
(vi) E.F.M. telegrams 2½d. (British Empire and many destinations where Forces are serving.)

Remittances may be sent by postal order, except to Canada, Newfoundland and U.S.A. Limit £2 2s. 0d. per remitter per day.

4. For particulars regarding CSN telegrams (allowed for urgent and private business) which may be sent only by next-of-kin, enquire—For Officers—

Under Secretary of State,
Air Ministry,
Department AR 8, London.

For Airmen—
A.O. I/c The Record Office,
Royal Air Force,
Barnwood,
Gloucester.

Yours **with love**

Signature **Don**

M22227 12/44 JC&S 702

big estate. He said he reduced height and, flying along the main drive, dived past the building. It was lunch-time and some of the office staff were outside the building, probably taking a short walk, when they were buzzed. However, being late in the War he imagined it would not occur to them that it was other than a friendly aircraft, and when he made a second pass, and several now waved, he knew they were not concerned. He said he had no doubt that it had livened up their quiet country existence that many had enjoyed for five years. Later that night he telephoned his wife and learnt that although she had heard a noise she had not bothered to go outside! Low flying was of course frowned upon and Dad said that earlier in the War his old friend Del had done the same thing over a built-up area, Peterborough, and had been reported and found himself given twenty-eight days in the glass-house! Dad excused himself by saying he kept well clear of the building and was miles out in the country – he was not reported – and he was only young.

A week or two went by and then one day whilst at a lecture in one of the huts on the drome, a sergeant entered, interrupted the lecture and announced postings. Some were to OTUs (Operational Training Units) and some Overseas. Dad was posted overseas which meant out East. He had only been back in England a matter of weeks and now here he was off again. He had been posted with the lads from Pensicola, and they were given a few days leave and told to report to Blackpool.

In Blackpool they were placed in a small hotel on the south side of town. Blackpool had been throughout the War a place full of RAF and these small hotels, still privately run, were used to house officers during their usually short stay in town. It was a typical small seaside hotel – really nothing more than a large terraced house, but no doubt the owners were on to a good thing. Hotels full in the winter months was obviously a bonus and many had RAF personnel from Monday to Friday, when many officers not posted would find their way home, and American servicemen at weekends, often using the same rooms and beds (and bedclothes!), with their girlfriends too as Dad said he found lipstick on his towel after one weekend away.

Dad and his friends had nothing to do whilst they were there except collect tropical kit and have the necessary inoculations required for an overseas posting.

He well remembers the Yellow Fever jab as this was carried out in a large hall with a stage. The recipients lined up below and filed on to the stage to be jabbed by the MO in front of the big audience awaiting their turn below. In those days the Yellow Fever jab had a very noticeable delayed action and it wasn't until a few seconds after the needle had struck that the sharp pain appeared, often just as one was leaving the stage, causing much amusement to the audience.

Dad learnt that they were not to be in Blackpool long and that one generally had twelve hours notice before leaving. Dad got in touch with his wife and arranged for her to join him in Blackpool for a few days. He booked a room in a small hotel a few doors away which had not been taken over by the RAF.

Chapter 18

Overseas Again

They had had only one or two days together in Blackpool when Dad was informed that the posting was on and that they would be leaving Blackpool station in the early hours of the next morning – about 4 a.m., Dad seems to remember. He duly arranged for his friends to make sure he was up and ready to go when it was time. The lads would make a noise outside his window which faced the street and wait until he appeared. Naturally it was a very traumatic time, to leave your new wife of a few weeks for an unknown destination not knowing whether you would meet again was bad enough but being at such an ungodly hour made everything seem so much worse. Dad says he was up and ready to go at the appropriate time and soon the lads were throwing stones up at the window and generally making a racket outside until he appeared. It was pitch dark outside, Dad said, reminding me that there was still a blackout in force. They duly parted at the hotel, Betty to return by train to London later that day. Soon Dad was on the special train that drove north towards the Clyde.

On this journey Dad said he and one or two of his friends shared a compartment with two Australians whom he got to know quite well. They became known by others as Laurel and Hardy – one was a very big fellow who had been a tree feller or lumberjack, whilst his colleague was quite small. Both were to be known as real terrors and not being at all keen on being told what to do.

Once again the port of departure was Greenock but this time it was not the mighty 'Mary' which waited out in the river but an old steamer called the *Cameronia*. On board they got settled in for the voyage but it didn't happen as quickly as it had on the 'Mary' – no, it was waiting for a convoy to be formed and it was a week before they finally sailed – one week stuck on board in the middle of the Clyde!

Eventually they sailed and when they got out into the open sea there were ships as far as the eye could see. On station next to Dad's ship was, most surprisingly, a ship he knew only too well and on which he had sailed some years earlier; it was H.M. Troopship *Dilwara*. In 1936 Grandad and Grandma had given up their holiday (Grandad only had one week's paid holiday a year), to let their son go on a school cruise which cost six guineas! The cruise had been to Portugal, Madeira and Casablanca (Dad has always said he was there before Humphrey Bogart) but had unfortunately not called at Gibraltar or Ceuta in Spanish Morrocco as the Spanish Civil War had just started and to avoid incidents, since Franco was pushing his troops across the Straits of Gibraltar to Spain, the Straits had been closed by the British Navy, or so they were told. The ship on which Dad had sailed was the *Dilwara*.

For days the *Cameronia* and *Dilwara* slowly sailed side by side until the convoy reached the Straits of Gibraltar when the old *Cameronia* set off on her own up the Med. Of course earlier in the War the worse would yet be to come and the convoys would continue right through to Egypt being pounded often all the way to Malta and beyond. However, now ships were unescorted as far as Malta when they did pick up an escort as there could be problems in the last part of the Med, the Germans still occupying Crete. There was no enemy action and Dad duly arrived in Port Said where they were told to disembark. They were still not sure where they were heading. They were taken to a transit camp under canvas just outside the town and on the banks of the canal. They were told they were not allowed to leave camp, which some ignored and went into town in the evenings. The two Aussies naturally went in and got very drunk returning late one night via the canal in a boat rowed by some poor Egyptian who had to suffer their shouting which all could hear, 'Row you bastard, row!' It seems they had wrecked part of the town and were being sought by Military Police when they escaped by canal. Luckily, Dad and all the others were shipped out next day by train.

The camp they left, Dad remembered, had many Italian prisoners of war who cooked and generally did all the chores in the camp. They were not it seemed restrained in any way – none Dad was told were too keen to escape as their life there was not too bad and in any case there was nowhere to go. North Africa had by then fallen to Monty.

The train south took them to El Cantara which was the crossing place of the canal. They arrived in the dark and were soon ferried across to another waiting train which left some hours later. Rumours, which had been persisting for some time, proved true; they were on their way up to

Palestine. The train was equally as slow as the one had been on the other side of the canal and the morning light revealed a complete wilderness which was the Sinai Desert.

The train journey was painfully slow but eventually Dad says they left the train at a place called Lydda from where they were taken by lorries, which almost at once started a climb. As they climbed, the hills became green which was in sharp contrast to the barren soil of the landscape below and towards Gaza and Sinai beyond, which they had earlier passed through. Indeed a land full of milk and honey Dad said. They were heading for Jerusalem and on arrival were taken to a building near the Jaffa Gate called the Italian Hospital which was to become their home for the next few months.

At that time, Dad reminded me, Palestine was under a British Mandate dating from the First World War. He said they soon learnt that although it was apparently peaceful there was some sort of trouble around underground. It was clear that those concerned were waiting for the War to end before coming out in the open and starting trouble. Groups of young Jewish boys marching in the streets dressed in khaki shorts became a common sight around the town – all very military.

Jerusalem was a transit centre for the RAF in the Middle East and Dad says there was not much to do there except wait for postings. He was crewed up for an expected posting to an OTU somewhere but no-one seemed to know too much. One just waited. There was quite a mixture of aircrew living in the hospital including a number of South Africans and one in particular sticks in Dad's mind as he was always playing the bagpipes. Dad later became friendly with another South African but most of those in the hospital were not liked and, no doubt having been fed with their own propaganda on the exploits of the 6th Armoured Division in the North African campaign, considered they had won the war in Africa. There was considerable ill feeling between them and Dad's friends.

Dad was reminded of the papers in Canada which often headlined, RCAF bombs Berlin or some other German city; the fact that the RAF probably made up four-fifths or more of the raid was not mentioned and one could get the impression that the Canadians alone were bombing Germany. It was understandable but also annoying particularly if you knew the score – of course both the Canadians and the South Africans did excellent work in the War but their press did perhaps give a slanted view. To put it in perspective, the population of Canada was only 11 million at that time and the whites in South Africa probably no more than 2 million – Britain's population was then some 48 million and there were 2 million in the RAF.

Jerusalem was a most interesting city: the mainly Jewish part was not much different from other Middle East or North African towns which had been influenced by Europeans, but the Old City was quite different and looked as if it had not changed since the days of the Bible. Dad was able to see all the places which nowadays are great tourist attractions and many days he and his friends wandered round the maze of streets which seemed never ending – in this part of the city there lived both Jews and Arabs, although he was told the majority there were Arabs.

He was also able to go to Bethlehem and was shocked to find that there was quite open commercialism around the place – even though there was a war or perhaps because there had been a war and many men to see the sights, there had grown souvenir shops. It was more like a holiday resort and not at all as he might have imagined. One of the shopkeepers even accepted a cheque from him for a bible he bought for his wife – this certainly surprised him since his cheque was on a London bank without any guarantee as there might be today. Obviously he was dealing with a keen businessman who knew when to take risks. Today of course no-one would think twice about there being souvenir shops but times were different then and the image of the Holy Land built up at school was so different from this.

One of his friends, Ron, was apparently a keen hockey player and he soon found a resident team made up, Dad believes, of RAF and Army personnel, who went under the name of The Scarabs. On one day when they were short Ron persuaded Dad to play for them which he did having only played once before when the school First XI football played their annual event against the local Girls High School First XI hockey – the boys had had only one practice match but had managed to win, Dad says, due to the brilliance of their then Captain, who he remembers as being one Eric Stevens.

He doesn't remember if he played more than once for the Scarabs.

Once again Dad was given leave whilst awaiting posting and this time he went down to Tel Aviv. Dad says the journey down to the plains was always quite hairy as the buses used to coast down much of the way to preserve petrol and relied solely on their brakes even though some of the road down was very steep.

Of course today Tel Aviv is so well known having been seen many times on television that it is difficult to imagine the initial impact it had on Dad at that time when he first saw it. It was clean with good streets and plenty of nice shops and a fine beach. Dad stayed at the Officers' Club which was right on the seafront. It was here he met a South African Army Officer who

Tel Aviv.

knew his way around and they became good friends, but Dad cannot now even remember his name, although he knows they had one or two enjoyable evenings together. The South African was streetwise and knew just how to get rid of the girls who waited outside the club much of the day. Dad learnt they were mostly German or Austrian Jews and undoubtedly found the Officers' Club the best place to ply their wares. 'Tell them to go away in Arabic; they don't like that as they take it as an insult,' so said the South African. This was done each time they left the Club and they got many rude remarks and gestures for their pains – Dad says he later found when on his own that it was not really necessary to be rude although they did take a bit of persuading that you weren't interested.

One day Dad says he got himself terribly burnt on the beach and in the evening turned bright red – he had never ever used sun-tan oil. In fact he had never before had occasion to just sit under a hot sun in shorts with his shirt off. He says he was there no more than half an hour but he was soon burnt – it was March!

Whilst in Tel Aviv he met a young lady in a shop and spent a few days with her. She was Jewish and lived the other side of Jaffa which adjoined Tel Aviv. One evening he accompanied her home in a taxi and much to Dad's surprise the driver spoke with a familiar Jewish Cockney accent – he had been a London taxi-driver before the War. Dad says it was easier going round with a local; she had been born in Tel Aviv and obviously came from quite a wealthy family. She took him to some very interesting places around Tel Aviv.

Back in Jerusalem the authorities organised a war game. Dad and a number of others were taken out of Jerusalem in a sealed lorry and dumped in the hills and told to find their way back and try to get into the city without being caught by the defenders who were made up of the remainder from the hospital.

They divided into two groups and Dad's group headed off down the nearby valley where one of the lads swore he had spotted train smoke. En route Dad remembers they passed a solitary Arab and to whom Ron, who had a few words of Arabic, greeted him politely. Still on high ground they all saw train smoke and hurriedly made their way down to find the inevitable railway line. In fact they found a small station or halt before the train arrived. Whether it was due to stop or not the engine driver must have been so surprised to see the 'crowd' gesturing that he slowed to a crawl which was a sufficient signal for the RAF to board in spite of the protestations of the guard who was obviously out of his depth in knowing how to cope with a bunch of RAF officers taking over his train. The train at least was going in the right direction and as it entered the built-up area they were able to wave at some of the outer city defenders whom they saw waiting idly by the rails. Dad's crowd jumped off as the train bumped across points before entering the station and they got back to the hospital without being captured. Not surprising, Dad added, since half the defenders were already back having got fed up with waiting. In retrospect, Dad said, it was all rather childish but it was good fun and it was quite an experience walking in the hills around Jerusalem.

So the waiting in Jerusalem went on. It then became general knowledge that Dad and his friends would be posted to Nicosia in Cyprus for conversion on Beaufighters – why exactly Beaufighters when they were crewed up for Sunderlands, etc., Dad doesn't remember. They talked about Japanese shipping strikes and how the Beaufighter swung badly on take-off but that was all he could remember.

Entertainment in Jerusalem consisted of the cinema, an occasional dance at the YMCA and the mess bar. Dad suddenly remembered that he had never told me that all officers there had a batman allocated to them. Dad's man, an Arab, was called Ahmed and Dad paid him by giving him all his cigarette ration which was much prized and marketable. At the cinema Dad said he remembers seeing *For Whom the Bell Tolls*, and said that on either side of the screen there were translations in Arabic and Hebrew which somehow ran in time with the film – he thinks!

Dad said he also met a Jewish girl who had escaped from Vienna and who told him that she attended meetings of an underground movement; she even offered to take him to one of the meetings. Dad said he told her that she and her friends had better not start anything or Tel Aviv would be flattened. 'Why do you think so many pilots are in Jerusalem?' he added. Of course at the time no-one was really aware of what trouble there would be there and how organised the Jews were – it was treated then as a bit of a joke by the uninformed RAF officers in the Italian hospital.

It was about this time that the young brother of Dad's school friend Charlie turned up in Jerusalem – he was the chap, Dad reminded me, who he had met in Saskatoon and who had by chance travelled back with him from Canada and came along to his wedding. Cyril was not on Dad's intake and therefore it was unlikely he would be on the same posting. Cyril told Dad that the last he had heard of Charlie was that he was with the fleet in the Far East. Charlie was a Fleet Air Arm pilot and sadly, as I may have mentioned earlier, Dad said, he was later killed.

Meanwhile the news from the War in Europe was good and it became obvious that that part of the War would soon be over. Of course everyone was well aware that the War in the East was by no means over and it had been shown that the Japanese were not easily dislodged from that which they had taken. None of the pilots in Jerusalem had any illusions as to where they would be heading and that it could be years before that War ended.

Exactly when his posting arrived he could not remember; was it before VE Day or just after. He thinks it must have been before as he cannot remember seeing the same faces around him in his blurred recollections of that night. The posting as expected was to Nicosia and yes it was to be for Beaufighters and, as they understood, Japanese shipping strikes. Two days before the posting Dad was taken ill and the MO put him in sickbay where he remained for over a week. He remembers his pals coming to see him just before they left for Nicosia but doesn't remember much else; he was, he said, pretty groggy.

Whether this was the last posting to Nicosia or whether the posting happened after VE Day Dad was vague. He does remember that young Cyril was present on VE night but then, if this was the last posting, how came Cyril ended up in Indo-China? Dad was obviously confused and imagined that Cyril must have still been in Jerusalem when Dad left if his friends from Pensicola had been posted whilst Dad was in hospital.

Chapter 19

VE Day! In Jerusalem and VE Day at Home

Dad might have been confused over the postings but he certainly was not confused when he remembered VE Day. Of course he would sooner have been in London but it seems they did quite a bit of celebrating in Jerusalem. It was something to remember. The Officer's Mess laid on free drinks for two days and as the majority of drink out there was of the short variety, beer being quite scarce, it was not difficult to see how very soon there was a good deal of merriment. Various antics were performed in the mess and one lad, who Dad said must have come off the stage or out of a circus performed a trick on a chair. The idea was for the occupant of the chair to lean backwards until the chair toppled and then spring over backwards and land on one's feet. It was performed by the lad several times to roars of approval from the audience and then Dad, who had had as he said quite enough to drink decided it was time someone else did the trick – it was so easy. That was his downfall. He told me that the chair went backwards OK and he managed to turn half a somersault but then the floor which, as most floors in a country where wood was scarce, was stone or tiled in stone, came up and hit him. Dad said he had a nice bruise and for some time afterwards was hardly in a fit state to walk – of course it caused great amusement all round.

That evening Dad said they went down to Zion Square and joined the crowd singing and shouting, mostly service people. The South African was there with his bagpipes and one shopkeeper who had a Union Jack hanging outside his shop nearly lost it when Dad hoisted on the shoulders of Lofty (one of his room-mates) tried to take it, but the pleas of the shopkeeper softened Dad and they left it alone. They then headed for the

169

YMCA where there was a dance in progress. Dad says he doesn't remember much of what happened but he was told after the War by his mother what he was supposed to have done. Young Cyril, who lived near to Dad's home, knew Grandma and visited her after the War. He had corresponded with her whilst he was in Indo-China, and had told her of the happenings of VE night in Jerusalem. As Grandma told Dad he was supposed to have taken an interest in an Arab girl at a dance (the YMCA). When he was seen talking to her, an Arab came up and drew a knife. Grandma told him that it was only with the help of his friends that Dad was dragged away from fighting the Arab with his bare hands.

It was some short time after VE night that Dad finally got his posting but unlike those who had gone to Cyprus, which they then knew was supposed to have been the last, he and those posted with him were not told where they were going except south to Egypt – 'Look at which way the boat is pointing when you get to Port Said' they were laughingly told.

They were driven in lorries down to Lydda and there boarded the train for Egypt. Dad only remembers one incident on that journey and that was when the train had to stop in the middle of nowhere while a poor camel driver tried to move his camel who had settled itself on the rails. They were held up about half an hour.

Dad doesn't remember how they got there but he said they ended up that journey at a camp on the side of the canal just outside Ismalia – it was an RAF camp called Cas Fereet.

Apart from a couple of trips into Ismalia Dad said he didn't remember anything much about the camp – he believes they had huts but really he didn't know; his mind was a complete blank. It is strange how some things remained in his mind quite clearly whilst other things had completely gone. He imagines it must have been a dump or he would have remembered, he said.

A few days later and they were entrained for Port Said but still no indication as to where they were to go thereafter. When arriving on the quay they soon knew which way they were going as over the side of the ship they saw hundreds of bronzed soldiers who, seeing the RAF officers, duly jeered them up the gangplank and on board. The soldiers were all wearing the familiar hats of the troops who had been out East. In fact these men had come from India having seen service with the 14th Army in Burma. The ship was full and Dad and the other RAF officers were put down in one of the holds which had been fitted out with bunk beds built high up towards the deck. Dad was given a bunk amongst officers of the 14th Army, all very good types who had been out east for nearly five years and were naturally glad to be on their way home. The ship, the *Carthage*, was well fitted out and although crowded managed to serve excellent meals for all aboard. The army, who had already been at sea a couple of weeks, put on an excellent concert party – much like, Dad said, the TV show many years later *It ain't arf hot Mum*. They performed on at least three nights and then there were films and lying on deck just watching the sea – it was great; he was on his way home and not out to the Far East. He could hardly believe his good luck – someone must have been watching over him, he said.

Now the German war was over there was no need for an escort and the Captain made the journey almost a cruise, particularly when he went in close to the North African coast to show everyone Carthage after which the ship had been named. For several hours one day Dad said they were 'escorted' by a French destroyer, the *Jean D'Arc* and there was much shouting between the two ships.

A week after leaving Port Said they dropped anchor at Gibraltar and there was much bartering done over the side of the ship, mostly with cigarettes as currency.

Dad said that either going out along the Med, but more likely coming back on the *Carthage*, they called in at Algiers – he could not remember why they called there but he knows they did.

Another week passed and they entered the Clyde which Dad remembers well as he said they had just gone down to lunch and were being served with steak and chips when the Captain announced over the Tannoy that they were now passing HM Battleship *Vanguard* – it was the first steak Dad had had since he left Canada and he was determined not to miss it. He said there was a general exit from the mess deck as scores went aloft to see the battleship, but Dad and a few other hungry men stayed with their steaks. In fact Dad says he in the end had three steaks – he never did see the *Vanguard*!

They duly docked in Glasgow and went by train to Harrogate and the familiar Queens Hotel.

Dad says you can imagine the surprise his wife had when he telephoned her to let her know he was back in England. He of course was given the customary disembarkation leave and they were able to take their belated honeymoon. They stayed a week in a small hotel/boarding house in Dawlish, South Devon. The place had been recommended to him by his old friend the leader of the band with whom he had earlier in the War acted as bouncer/doorkeeper. Don Varnier had stayed at the same place a few years earlier when Dad had been part of a RAF gymnastic display given there in the park during a Wings for Victory week – Dad said that Don always remembered the sergeant falling through the platform.

Mrs Bacon served excellent meals and, apart from Betty getting terribly sunburnt whilst on the beach, (Dad by this time was very brown having as they say, got some in overseas, and thus not affected) they had an excellent holiday. He said the journey down to Dawlish he remembers well and typical of wartime travel. He had booked first-class tickets but they had to spend the whole journey from Paddington to Exeter sitting on their cases in the corridor – the train was packed.

VE Day at Home

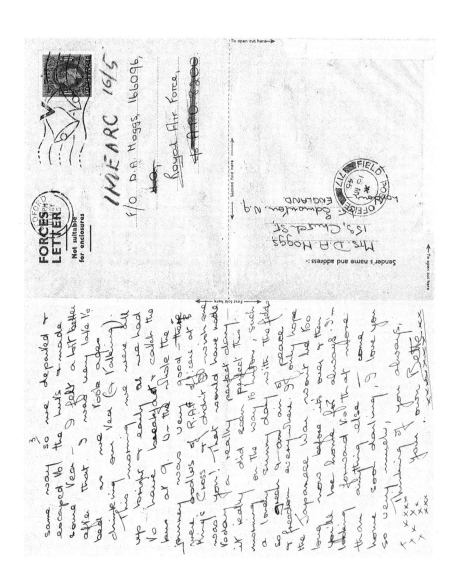

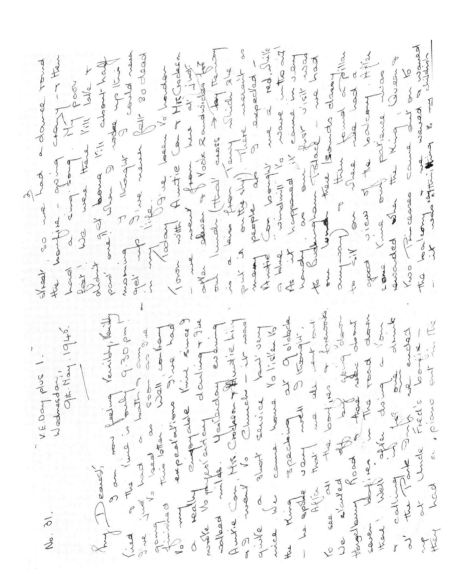

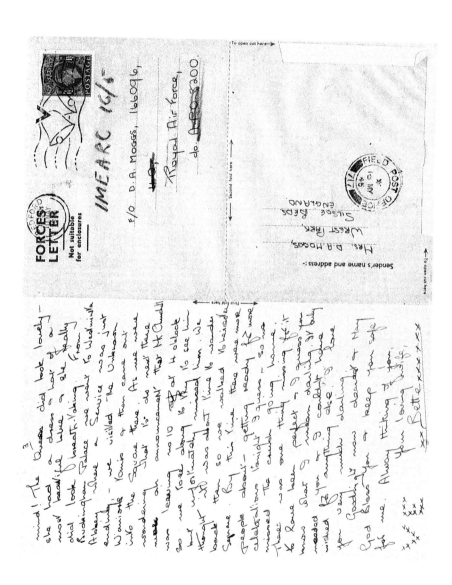

3 Park Avenue
Bush Hill Park
10. 5. 45.

Dear Don,

Well Don peace at last so no more rockets I can hardly believe it, we have got our flags flying & every street have had bonfires & dancing till the morning, the children have been clearing our to U2 site to get wood to burn. I hope we shall soon beat the japs then all the boys will be home, of course it must be bad for those that have lost husbands & sons now is the time they will realize it more. I thought about Mrs Horner, Mrs Illingworth has still not heard yet about the boys I called to ask on Ve day. Mrs Abrahams son is home he came last Sunday week but I've not seen him yet. She says he is very thin & must rest a while. I received your letter of the 1st am glad you are better & was able to have your leave so you have Cyril with you & your other

Extract of letter from Dad's mother – my grandma I don't remember.

Chapter 20

Battle Course and Football

On return from leave it was back to Harrogate and then shortly after a posting to Credenhill, Hereford, for a battle course. Dad was there for a month and went through arduous training with the RAF Regiment – over assault courses in full pack and rifles, building bridges and derricks, the rifle range and simulated battles with long route marches. He remembers how their group was nearly always accompanied on their marches with a Scottish piper. He managed to get home twice during the course leaving on the Saturday afternoon by train to Paddington but, and this is something I think worth mentioning, because of no suitable trains to Hereford on the Sunday, the return journey was made from Euston late at night, changing at Crewe and catching a milk train down to Hereford arriving about 5 a.m. The things one did to get home for a while! Dad said he was to do this journey again when posted once again to Hereford, but that was later. The battle course was, as expected, tough but Dad was very fit in those days and he cannot remember anything bothering him. He did remember how a sergeant shouted at him when he appeared though a pipe, which passed under a road and was full of water, carrying his rifle, which he had accidentally dropped, with water pouring from the barrel – he laughed at the memory but would not repeat what the sergeant called him.

Another incident he remembers was when they were on a big exercise and had to get to camp somewhere along the Wye. He and his air-gunner friend he had made on the course called in a couple of pubs on the way and after a few drinks decided to surprise a cyclist they saw coming down the empty country lane. They had just reached a thick forest section of the road and concealed themselves at the side of the road, and when the cyclist passed they fired two blanks. The man nearly fell off his bicycle,

got off and turned around. They remained hiding, but much to Dad's surprise he recognised the man – it was his French teacher from a school he had left in 1937. The man must have been on a cycling holiday. Dad says he regrets not speaking to him but was too ashamed at what they had just done and kept in hiding until he left.

I found an interesting item in one of Dad's letters at about this time. Writing to his wife he first mentions his air-gunner friend, who it turned out was a country boy, and says 'Eddie brought back some eggs and tomatoes with him – we went along to the mess and with our breakfast had them fry a couple of eggs for us . . .' and then later, 'By the way if I should get home next week and if Eddie gets home as well, then he'll probably be able to get me some tomatoes and maybe a few eggs and a cucumber – you could come with me to the Manor House and meet him there with me on my way back – and then you could carry the stuff back with you . . .' It shows how there was rationing and how prized eggs and tomatoes were at that time.

After the final big exercise which had ended the day after the cyclist incident there was just one more day before the course ended and they were due for a spot of leave before reporting back to Harrogate. They were in their hut packing their bags ready to leave camp when the small radio owned by one of the lads announced that a bomb, called an atom bomb, had been dropped on a town in Japan and terrible devastation had been caused. It was new to all present but from the radio announcement they soon were made to realise that the war against Japan might fast be coming to an end.

Dad said it was difficult to imagine the feeling amongst the men. The war in the Far East had obviously for some time been going better with the 14th Army pushing the Japs out of Burma and the Americans capturing island after island in the Pacific and had already captured Okinawa which, although some couple of hundred miles from mainland Japan, was nevertheless considered by the Japanese as part of Japan. However, even with all this progress it was considered the War was still a long way from over, but now things seemed to have changed and it was likely there would be a dramatic end.

The next day Dad was off to his home, which now was two rooms at the top of his mother-in-law's house, and a few days leave. The War ended as all know after the dropping of a second atom bomb on Nagasaki and Dad was at home for VJ Day. Living in North London he easily made his way up to the West End to join in all the celebrations as he had done in Jerusalem a few months earlier – but this time he was sober!

The leave over it was back to Harrogate and then a posting to Market Harborough where Dad and his colleagues were kept occupied by lectures and interviews on what to do after leaving the services and whether to study. There of course were marches and brushes with the RAF Regiment but, having recently been trained with them at Credenhill, Dad and his friends from the Hereford camp were often excused. It seems he managed to get home once or twice at weekends. Apart from the activities mentioned and the occasional church parade there was also football, of a very high standard it seems, and a lot of cross-country running.

At first Dad didn't get a place in the station team but after a couple of weeks it seems he was in. From Dad's letters I can see that football and cross-country running played a large part in the activities on the station; it was not just football at weekends but almost every day, or so it seems. An extract from one of Dad's early letters on this camp indicates the footballing standard. 'Tomorrow afternoon I am going to Kettering with the football team. Unfortunately for me I am not playing – I am reserve. We have a strong side, there are about a 1,000 bods to choose from, and the fellow who is playing inside-left is a professional – he is playing for Walsall on Saturday – he is a sergeant PTI. Our outside-left is a professional too – he is a corporal and is playing for Huddersfield on Saturday, I have been told they will find me a place next week but meanwhile travel as 12th man.'

The cross-country races were very keenly fought as invariably forty eights would be awarded for the winning flight and all those who came in the first ten. Dad who had always done well at school in cross-countries always managed to get in the first ten.

Another extract, 'We had a game of football this morning – our flight played a flight of sergeants, I quite enjoyed the game even though it was one sided, funny enough the score was again 7–1, the same as the station match last week – however this time I scored six of the seven goals. I have been selected to play for the station team tomorrow afternoon against RAF Desford – we have a pretty strong side . . .'

The letter from which the above was taken goes on to talk about the demob speed-up announced by the Government, but Dad and his friends did not think too much of it and says, 'At that rate I will be in another two years . . .' It seems it rankled that the Navy demob was going to be much quicker.

On this station he had to take his turn as Orderly Officer and that meant being there over the weekend and inspecting the various messes and witnessing the weighing of the meat, etc. in the main stores. Then the fire picquet had to be paraded and inspected, the ensign raised and lowered, the post office keys collected, etc, etc. Obviously an onerous job which Dad was pleased to lose.

It was at Market Harborough that he played football with a George Pearce who just before the War had played on the Corinthians World Tour and thus was with Cass Braithwaite who had formed the band that Dad had gone around with early in the War – Cass had played with St Albans and Dad still had a Corinthian's team photo he had been given a few years earlier.

Several matches were played at that station but one Dad remembered well was when they played away at a nearby station, Husbands Bosworth. Dad says a good crowd watched the game and for most of it he was barracked by a group of fellows from the home station whom he soon recognised as ex-colleagues from the Middle East. At first he couldn't hear what they were saying until he heard the word Jerusalem, 'Send old Moggs back to Jerusalem, send him off!' was the cry. It was all a bit of a laugh Dad said and he actually said he enjoyed being barracked.

Some weeks later and after many games of football, sometimes three in a week, and many cross-countries, he was posted on a swimming course to Blackpool! The course consisted of the usual RAF dinghy drills and improving swimming – Dad says he had a good time whilst there. He then went back to Market Harborough.

From Dad's letters it seems that there were a number of postings soon after he got back to the satellite drome at Husbands Bosworth but because of football Dad was held back. He remained at the same station until the year end and, judging by letters, was playing football almost daily, the majority of which seem to have been away from home. It was obvious the RAF had to keep everyone busy and playing and watching football matches in the winter was a good way of passing time.

It was in January 1946 that Dad was eventually posted to Husbands Bosworth and he with others were officially told they were now redundant as aircrew. From that station one of his letters says they would be sent to a redundancy board and then posted to Pembrey in South Wales to await a posting to another job. His main recollection of Husbands Bosworth was how cold it was in the huts and before posting he played for the station at football.

Dad had started a correspondence course with Bennetts College of Sheffield: older people he said would remember their, 'Let me be your father', and had already started sending back lessons.

I asked Dad how he felt about being made redundant. He said he had joined the RAF to do his bit and as the War was now over he had no great desire to carry on flying and really he with many others were just anxious to get back to normality and into civvy street, particularly so as they were just wasting time; he was now twenty-four and the War had started when he was seventeen. Through various circumstances he had missed all the operational postings both at home and overseas – all that training and not used. However, as he said to me later, there have been thousands of RAF pilots trained since the War and apart from the few in the Korean and Falklands War none had done any more than he had.

Redundant – this was the first use of the word that Dad had become familiar with in his life although he told me it was to become a word in common usage in later years when someone thought it would be a kinder word to use for people about to be sacked from their employment. They even brought in a law to 'protect' redundants but it really gave the excuse to lots of employers to push people out they would never have done before the Act was passed.

A short posting to Eastchurch on the Isle of Sheppey was followed by the move to Pembrey in South Wales. This station, another holding depot, was little different from the previous two he had been at – hundreds of officers and other ranks being kept occupied with lectures, parades and more lectures. He said he managed to get on with his correspondence course and visit Llanelly, the nearest town from time to time. The latter known to servicemen as Slash. . . .

Having been told at Husbands Bosworth they were to be made redun dant the official line was given to them at Pembrey. All aircrew not on operational squadrons would be grounded. NCOs would be reduced in rank to Leading Aircraftmen (LACs), which Dad said was most unfair and degrading to have to lose their stripes, whilst Officers would be given a choice as to the groundwork to be followed. The release procedure from the services had been carefully worked out by the powers that be and it seemed that Dad had about another year to go before he would likely become eligible for release. He was given the following from which to choose – adjutant, administration officer, motor transport officer, or ac-countant officer. Since Dad had worked in an office before and in the early years of the War when people had tried to get him to study for an accountancy qualification, it seemed reasonable that he chose to train as an Accountant Officer.

He stayed at Pembrey awaiting his posting to the RAF School of Administration and Accountancy and of course played football for the station. He said he well remembers one game against a mining village team, Ponthenry he thinks the place was called. The people of the village which was some miles inland from the camp, looked after them well but Dad remembers how poor everyone looked – Dad's team won the match and he remembers that it was one of the only occasions in his footballing career that he genuinely felt sorry they had won.

Chapter 21

Administration and Accountancy

The RAF School of Administration and Accountancy had been located at Hereford, so once again he found himself at Credenhill with the difficult journey back on a Sunday night after a weekend at home.

The course was very comprehensive. It lasted nine weeks, and at the end there were examinations which Dad duly passed. He thinks he then went back briefly to Harrogate before being posted to a station as the Assistant Accountant Officer. The station was Hawarden near Chester but just over the border in North Wales.

Hawarden was a happy posting and he learnt a great deal there. The Senior Accountant Officer was a Squadron Leader, which was the rank for the post, who had only a short time to go before his release. Most RAF Accountant Officers in the War were qualified accountants and a good deal older then the average aircrew and thus were due for a relatively early release. The staff at Hawarden soon accepted Dad, the new boy, and as the only aircrew in the offices became very popular with the WAAF's and respected by the male Pay and Stores clerks. Aircrew, Dad said, whether pilot, navigator, air bomber or gunner, were always held as something different from ground staff – particularly by the fairer sex and of course of all aircrew the pilot was the most glamorous to be.

The work of the accountant included payment of all airmen, airwomen and non-commissioned officers. This was generally by a formal pay parade unless pay had to be sent to a small station where numbers did not warrant this procedure. There was such a posting at Harwardan and one of early jobs Dad was given was the run out to Hooton Hall in Cheshire where there were one or two airmen and no doubt a sergeant or corporal who were to receive their pay from Harwarden. Dad remembers the ride across the Wirral with some pleasure. However, he could not remember what they did

R.A.F. SCHOOL OF ADMINISTRATION AND ACCOUNTANCY.

Vivian of Hereford

No. 76 ACCOUNTANT OFFICER'S COURSE SYND " E " 20-2-46—3-4-46.

F/O R. S. Junor   F/L N. W. Lenton   F/O J. C. Littlejohns   F/O A. Mennan   F/O D. A. Moggs   P/O J. R. Mungall   F/L A. Musson
F/O P. H. T. Fardon

F/O A. L. Ford   F/O I. A. B. Galletly   P/O K. J. Gibb   F/O R. Grove   F/O D. Gunn   F/O J. M. Hall   F/O J. H Haslam
F/O F. C. Hudson   F/O C. M. Husband   F/O G. R. Jenkins.

F/O A. C. Chilvers   F/O B. R. Clarke   F/O E. Creasey   F/O T. B. Daniels   F/O C. F. Dashwood   F/L L. Eagle
F/O G. E. Etherington   F/O F. K. Evans   F/O C. Eyre   F/O J. Farquharson.

F/O H. N. Ash   P/O G. Beardmore   F/O E. Beaumont   F/L R. Dyer   F/L K. H. Deane   F/O J. Bilsland   F/O S. R. Cave.

at Hooton Hall but it was, he knows, the first time he identified a Liverpool accent – no doubt he had heard it before but this time, he says, he was talking to one of the airmen he had just paid and, noticing the strong accent, had asked where he came from. The other airmen nearby laughed, probably at such a ridiculous question, and the man pointed across the river, the River Mersey, which was clearly visible from Hooton. Of course with the advent of TV and the Beatles, Liverpool accents are well known to all but at that time, Dad said, unless you had been there or been told, it was not so easy for a mere Southerner to locate an accent.

Harwarden was also the graveyard of many operational planes. There were hundreds of bombers lined up on one part of the station and Dad often wonders why so few are now around – someone did not have much vision. He supposed everyone was so fed up with the war that they were glad to get rid of them – but what would they be worth today!

It was while at Harwarden that Dad recounted an amusing incident that occurred when he hitched a ride on a plane home for a weekend. It seems an Anson, a kite which Dad was all too familiar with, was flying down to Hendon and as Dad had no duties that Saturday thought he would see if the pilot would take him as a passenger. When it was agreed and Dad got aboard he found he was not alone – already seated were two young airmen who themselves had managed to get a lift. Remember Dad was an officer with wings and twenty-four years old; these two lads looked about eighteen and very new.

They took off and were soon in cloud and then above. They were not flying high and every now and again the cloud cover below broke and there was a glimpse of the ground. The air became very bumpy particularly as they began to fly at the base of heavy cumulus cloud. Dad said he could see the two young airmen feeling unsettled and gradually getting sick, so he handed them bags. He said he felt for them but he himself had not a clue where they were, and therefore how much further they had to go. Suddenly he spotted ahead a very familiar building, Luton Town Hall, and knew just where they were. Just then one of the airmen looking decidedly green spoke up, 'Can you tell us, sir, how much longer we will be before we land?'

'Oh, not long now,' Dad said he happily replied. 'We are just passing over Luton and in a minute or two you will see St Albans' Cathedral – we'll be down in 10 minutes,' he said, reassuringly, just as if he had known all the time where they were. Dad said he chuckled inwardly but felt he had not let the side down and at least given these young men confidence in their officers – if they did but know!

It was then that Dad said most people who fly today do not know what it is like to be airsick; oh yes, sometimes on short flights and when circling low around airports sickness can occur but nowadays planes fly at heights which are above turbulence and it must seem strange that many men were 'washed-out' through airsickness. A great deal of flying when Dad was a pilot was always in turbulence and airsickness was not uncommon.

Dad obviously had happy memories of this station and referred once or twice to one or two evenings in the local pub and in visits to Chester.

A few months after arriving the Senior Accountant Officer was given his release date and Dad was primed to take over from him as Acting Squadron Leader – unfortunately men were being released throughout Maintenance Command and without thinking of the forthcoming loss of the senior at Hawarden, Air Ministry wanted Dad elsewhere. First he was posted to Bristol, this was cancelled just before he was all set to go and was changed to an urgent posting to a drome in Northamptonshire.

It was not unusual for posting to be changed as Dad found prior to going to Harwarden when he had been sent down to Andover and after duly arriving was told they did not know he was coming – someone had blundered!

However, the posting to Northamptonshire looked as if it were going to happen. The whole of Pay and Stores Accounts turned out for a farewell party at the local and Dad said goodbye to many good friends he had made in such a short time.

His posting was to a Maintenance Unit and Ferry Pool using a drome that the RAF had not long before taken over from the Americans. The station was twelve miles outside Peterborough and right out in the country near to the villages of Oundle (famous for its school) and Polebrook. The station was called Polebrook. The previous Accountant Officer was still on station but was only to be there three days before his release. So in three days Dad said he had to get familiar with looking after a station – a very short time when he would be responsible for all headquarters' block. He had to rely on the NCOs to guide him through his difficulties. Then there was the Commanding Officer, a Squadron Leader and an ex-air-gunner. For those who knew the devil-may-care attitude of many air-gunners this gentleman was no exception – a good type, very streetwise, to use a modern expression. Dad had a few tales to tell me of what happened at this station.

Being an ex-American drome the accommodation was good, the Officer's Mess had a nude painted on the wall behind the bar and all round the walls were painted a record of every raid carried out by the Yanks at

CLEARANCE CERTIFICATE.

Sub Form
578

Rank....F/o........ Name and Number... MOGGS. D. A. ....Branch.... GD/Accts.
1660096.

DEPARTMENT	SIGNATURE	DATE.
Flight or Section	_____ F/o	12/6/46
Station Adjutant (F.1369)	RAArthur Weedham S/L	12/6/46
P.2. Clerk - S.N.O.	M. Shark; Cpl.	12/6/46
Armament Officer.	J. Jordan F/o.	
Officer i/c Parachutes.	J.C. Ben Plt.	
Anti Gas Officer.	N/A	
Sports Officer.	WP Sawbury Flt	12/6/46
Equipment Section (Form 667B MUST be produced)	A. Lyle. Sgt. 12/6/46.	
Cobblers Shop.	Mc Gr...	12/6/46.
Station Sick Quarters.	G.W. Watt. Sac pp 140	12.6.46.
Education Officer.	D.R. Morgan F/Lt.	12.6.46.
Officers' Mess Library.	E.Rumer	12-6-46
Officers' Mess.	E.Rumer	12-6-46
Officer i/c Secret & Confidential Publications.	RAArthur Weedham F/L	12-6-46
N.C.O. i/c Cycles	B. ...one. 12/6/46.	
Signals Section.	A.B. Lee F/o 12/6/46	
M.T. (Including Repayment Charges)	W/O Connelly 12/6/46	
Station Post Office	L. Henderson F/S	
Stores Accounts	_____ S/L	
Pay Accounts		

CERTIFIED that I have no publications, books etc., in my possession other than
those of personal issue.
Date.....12th June 1946   Signature......DMoggs F/o.........

DEFICIENCIES.

....
....
....
    LIABILITY ADMITTED.............   ....(Signature)
    Total number of hours flown as (pilot...............................
                          (a member of an air crew other than pilot.....
....   (hours have been flown during last six months;
of which ....

POSTED TO:-   251 M.U. Bristol.   W.E.F. -

CERTIFIED THAT THE DEFICIENCIES AND OTHER CLAIMS ARE RECORDED IN THE ACCOUNTING
SECTION AS CHARGEABLE TO..

A clearance certificate for a posting to Bristol that never happened.

Polebrook, with each date accompanied by painted Swastikas indicating the number of planes they claimed to have shot down. The RAF officers of course made some rude remarks about the latter but they were allowed to stay. Many of the officers' huts had names of the occupants still in place – amongst which was Major Clark Gable.

The station housing a Ferry Pool had many pilots around so the mess was often well occupied, often by strangers from other pools – the snooker table was in use much of the day although Dad says he was working most of the time and became envious of those in the Pool.

Dad seemed to be vague as to how many pay parades took place but he remembers it was Friday, either every week or every other week. The Station Accountant Officer took the parade, or rather the SWO (Station Warrant Officer) organised it and Dad as the Accountant paid out the money. For those who are not familiar with the then RAF procedures it apparently went as follows:

The Pay Account Clerks had previously prepared the pay due for each member of the station, that is all other than officers who were paid through a bank by Air Ministry Accounts, and had this detailed on the payroll sheets with pay due written in pencil against the name and number of the airman or WAAF as the case may be. On the Accountant Officer, accompanied by two witnessing officers, entering the hanger or some other place for the parade, the parade is brought to attention and the Station Warrant Officer or other NCO in charge salutes and as the officers sit the parade is stood at ease. The Station Accountant Officer has previously visited the bank to collect the cash and when seated stacks this in front of him.

The Pay Clerk calls out the name of the first person to be paid and that person comes to attention and sings out his last three, e.g., Pay Clerk shouts, 'LAC Jones D.R.' Jones coming to attention replies, '757, sir', and immediately leaves the ranks and comes forward for his pay, showing his identity card to the SWO or NCO in charge before visiting the pay table. In the meantime the Pay Clerk will have checked that the last three sung out by the man matches the number in the book and calls out the pay due, 'Two pounds four shillings' – the RAF, Dad seems to remember, paid out only in two shillings. The amount in pencil on the payroll is inked in and the Accountant counts the money and lays it on the table where it is collected by the man who returns to his place in the ranks. One Witnessing Officer sits by the side of the Pay Clerk and makes sure he acts correctly whilst the other sits by the side of the Accountant Officer and checks the correct amount is paid. Unfortunately it didn't always work like that; you could not rely on the witnessing officers as many didn't bother to check and were often, Dad said, looking at the WAAFs instead of the payroll and money.

At the end of the parade the officers and pay clerks would leave and the parade dismissed.

Dad said he soon got into a routine and as a convenient fast train to London left Peterborough, twelve miles away, with little time to spare he said he sometimes did not bother to see if what was left in cash balanced with what had been paid out – he left this to his NCOs to balance for him.

It was after one of these pay parades that Dad recalled his first instance of what he believed was telepathy – of course he did not consider it telepathy at the time but happenings many years later convinced him this is just what it was.

He left the station in a hurry after such a parade and travelled home on weekend leave. That night he went to bed in the usual way but in the morning his wife told him that he had got up in the night, switched on the light and started looking in the dressing-table drawers. When she asked him what he was looking for he had replied quoting a sum of money. She had said she realised from the way he spoke that he was sleepwalking and told him to get back into bed, which he did. Next morning he remembered nothing and did not think any more about it until, arriving back at the station and going into Pay Accounts, he was greeted with the fact that on Friday they had not been able to balance. Dad asked them what was the difference and they had told him they were £4. 8s. short. It was then Dad said he remembered what his wife had told him and resolved to ring her to see if she remembered the amount he had said he was looking for in the night. It was easy to contact her as she was a telephonist and he soon got through to her and asked her the question – she immediately replied £4. 8s.!

The difference was of course soon located and turned out to be no more than the clerk failing to ink in a payment made of £4. 8s. – the story of Dad and his sleepwalking caused some amusement but was no doubt soon forgotten. However, years later happenings which are not relevant to this study caused him to recall the above incident and it goes down in Dad's mind as a telepathic transfer to his subconscious by the NCOs when trying to achieve a balance for him.

Other happenings on the station also made good stories after the War, for example, the CO renting out blister hangers to the local farmers and asking Dad as the Station Accountant if it were all right to share the spoils between the messes. Dad who had been warned by Command about certain things did not wish to become involved and simply said, 'Yes it is quite in order if you have Air Ministry approval for the lettings.' To which the rely came, 'Oh Air Ministry know noting about this.' Then there was the woman, who lived on the camp with the CO, called by all Josephine, and then the closing down of stations and the acquisition of their remaining stock of liquor – stations were closing down all over the country at this time and there was hardly time to drink all stocks before a closing at short notice. Dad says he had often wondered what happened to this CO – he certainly was a character and I think Dad secretly admired the way he operated – perhaps he became a millionaire, who knows!

Daily parades were held outside Headquarters and these were some-times delegated to Dad to take – he was now twenty-four and he had through the War assumed a far greater responsibility than he had ever dreamed possible.

On one occasion Dad says he upset the SWO (Station Warrant Officer) who accompanied him on inspection of the men on parade. Walking along behind one of the ranks Dad says he came across a particularly scruffy airmen who looked as if he had not had a haircut for weeks. Dad says he touched the man's back and said, 'Haircut', whereupon the SWO sprang into action to take the man's name and number which he would have written in his little book but for Dad stopping him – Dad realised his mistake right away and the look on the SWO's face he still remembers. Whether the man got his hair cut Dad doesn't know but he said he did not want to get the man into trouble but simply to get his hair cut.

Also whilst at Polebrook he remembers going with the CO to close down a station near Sandy in Bedfordshire, a station called Tempsford. It was really a routine inspection to see with, Dad assumed, that station's SWO that all was secure and everything cleared from stores, etc.

Near to his final release from the service a big mess dinner was held when wives were invited. He booked a room in an hotel in Peterborough and his wife came up by train from London – he remembers how con-cerned she was as to what to wear – remember clothes were rationed and she had only been seventeen when war started. However, it seems all went very well and the guest of honour, Air Commodore . . . and his wife spent most of the evening, when dancing followed, in the company of Dad and Betty. Looking back Dad says it was like a dream. He has several times tried to remember how it must have been, dining with a large number of RAF officers with their ladies in the Officers' Mess with the huge nude over the bar and the record on the walls of all those 'missions' by the

Yanks over enemy territory. Perhaps, he said, they covered the nude, but he doesn't really remember.

Those were the days, he said, but he hadn't then prepared himself for the shock to come when he returned to civvy street and the Water Board.

Chapter 22

Demobilisation

Towards the end of 1946 Dad was given his release date and told to report to Uxbridge for demob. First he had to make sure some new Joe was available to take over from him on the station, and sure enough a couple of days before he was due to leave along came a bewildered young man who would soon be deeply involved in the affairs of this somewhat remote station.

Dad could not remember much about his last day at Polebrook. There was so much to do, he said, that one did not have the time to think or become emotional. In fact Dad said he had really only people who worked for him in the Admin building to say his farewells to – plus of course the CO. Other officers on the station being mainly ferry pilots were sometimes there and sometimes not – they were just snooker and the odd drink acquaintances.

He duly reported to Uxbridge and once there was soon fitted out with a cheap-looking suit plus the mandatory hat – a trilby, which he never wore. He could use his uniform until his demob leave was ended when he would officially leave the services. Extra leave and pay was given for overseas service and this plus the standard entitlement meant Dad had about three months to get used to being a civilian. At the end of his leave it would be five years since he was first given his RAF number and over six years since he first volunteered for aircrew duties. Being young, having wings and with the rank of Flight Lieutenant (for those unfamiliar with RAF ranks this is the equivalent to a Captain in the Army) he was not unnaturally somewhat proud of his achievement and knew all too soon he would be working in a junior capacity in the office he had left a few years earlier, whereas a short while ago he had been looking after twenty or thirty men and women doing work at least equivalent to that which he would shortly

194

find himself doing. It was therefore with some apprehension that he eventually put on his civvies. Yes, he returned to work during his leave and, at the request of one of the older women, he actually went in one Saturday morning in his uniform (in those days you had to work Saturday mornings in offices) and followed this up by walking up the road to the Spurs for the afternoon match. He remarked that on this occasion it had not got him a free seat as had happened a few weeks earlier when he and his wife had been given two seats near the directors' box by a complete stranger whilst they were queuing outside to get in – yes, an officer's uniform with wings was very highly respected in those days.

The uniform and rank he had held of course made no difference at his office. There were a number who had had just as much experience and many who had seen action and achieved high ranks. At Dad's small branch office in Tottenham only three of the original staff of seven had been young enough to be called to the fighting services and one older man was later required to work on the railways. Of the three younger men, the oldest was killed as an Observer in the RAF, the second became a lieutenant in the Navy and commanded a minesweeper for much of the War, and the youngest, was Dad, who went as office junior and returned as such. The first job he remembers being given was to stick some notices on the windows of the public office in the front saying 'WASTE NOT – WANT NOT'. He has laughed a lot about it since and, even though his war contribution was minimal, it came home to him how soon people's attitudes change and how soon they forget. He said he was reminded of his childhood and the scores of men who were forced to beg for money after fighting in the First World War. He told me that it was nothing to see men standing on the curb shaking uncontrollably or blind, selling matches or walking in the middle of the streets in the East End singing and hoping that the other poor of West Ham would give them a copper to get something to eat – 'Yes, son,' he said, 'we all soon forget and don't want to know – it's human nature and after all everyone has his own troubles.'

Chapter 23

Conclusion

Of course being out of the services never quite lived up to expectations especially as for the next few years things in the UK would be very hard. There was still rationing and even in 1952 when Dad had enough money to buy a car his enquiry at the Motor Show concerning the new Consul was met with, 'Of course there is a five year waiting list!' No, it was not easy in those first years after the War, he said.

Some years later (in fact it was, I discovered, twenty-six years) shortly after the death of his wife, Betty, Dad says he returned with my elder brother to his last RAF station – just to see what it was like. Well he is sure he found the place but instead of the gate, buildings and blister hangers, there was a field of corn with the remnants of one or two huts standing in the middle. No gates, no runway, in fact nothing to show that hundreds of Americans and later British airmen had walked those fields, lived and died there, caught the run to Peterborough, collected their pay, scived, fiddled and worked. Dad said, 'It gives you a funny feeling inside when you return. I don't suppose you should really, but something gets you to want to go back, just to show someone where you had been in those long-forgotten days of half a century ago.'

Dad also went back to Canada in later years and looked at two of the stations he was on, hoping to meet someone he knew. Of course he didn't and was it worth the visit – apparently he took my mum (his second wife) and me but I was only three so I don't remember any of it. I would like to go now. I can understand it now. I have lived the trauma through Dad, first of the London Blitz, the time when he learnt his friend Bob had been killed, his struggle to get into aircrew having a suspected heart problem and a blocked nose, his final acceptance, his first solo, his shipment to Canada and his seasickness, his endurance in getting his wings, his

196

marriage and being bombed on his wedding day and the little girl he took from the bombed house opposite, his posting out East and the night he left Blackpool with his friends throwing stones up at his window, the expected posting on Japanese shipping strikes, his illness and return to England, his battle courses, his accountancy courses and his work as an RAF Accountant Officer. No Dad, not a war that rates for medals for bravery, like Grandad in the First World War, but a war nevertheless, with all the emotions of leaving home and the courage needed to fly and being prepared to fight for one's country – it was no fault of yours you did not see action but, like the thousands of airmen who did, had it been your lot you would have done it too. Dad said he never really worried about the end result of his training; he was more concerned with getting his wings and whether his weak stomach would let him down – it didn't.

His story is told mainly as a record of what happened to one young man in a long war and to try to show what it was like to live at that time. I am sure he did not embellish; some would have shot a terrible line. After all who would be able to check, but Dad always seemed mildly embarrassed when drawn into war experiences until he had made it clear that, even though a pilot and in the RAF for five years, he was no hero and hadn't much to tell. Not much to tell, eh – well, enough for a book!

Thanks for telling me Dad but I am still not sure what to say if asked, 'What did your dad do in the War?'

Appendix

Old Friends

Dad is now over seventy and Mum chides him often that he has no friends, but when I look back at the many references to friends in his letters to Betty and then see the letters he has kept from comrades in the RAF, I begin to know my dad was not always the stick in the mud he often now appears to be. I asked Dad to tell me a little about his wartime friends and what happened to them and I asked him if he had kept in touch with any since the War.

His first friends in the War were those he knew from school and reference has been made earlier to some of these. Bob with whom he went on a cycling holiday was killed as shown earlier, and Del after over sixty raids over enemy territory was shot down and spent the rest of the War in a POW camp. Eric, not mentioned earlier, but equally one of the gang, became a fighter pilot and sustained severe injuries when his plane crashed in Yugoslavia. Bill, another of the gang, also became a pilot and was shot down over France and was smuggled over the Pyrenees by the French Resistance and got back to England via Gibraltar.

After the War Del managed a pub for a while in Barnet and Dad saw him over there a couple of times but has heard nothing from him for over forty years. He lost touch with the other two during the War.

His friend Ron who was on ground staff in the RAF and became his best man is the only one he has kept in touch with – he has long since retired as a Head Teacher. Dad has only seen him twice in the last twenty years.

The friends he made in the RAF have been lost to him since the War. He said somehow it seemed all different when back in civvy street and the promises made of meeting up were never kept – it's a bit like making friends on holiday, 'We must look you up when we get back', but how often does one.

198

6th March 1945,

P.P.S- If you see any of the boys, please remember me to them.

P/o Green. J. G.
No 165947
R.A.F. Station
Nassau
Bahamas
B.W.J

Hi! Don,

You've no idea how pleased I was to receive your letter just now. I've been thirsting for news of you ever since I came here. I'm glad you did'nt forget me, pal, I've thought about you a great deal and wondered if things turned out O.K for you when you arrived home.

Well, first of all, I will try to answer some of your numerous questions. Ernie and myself are on the same course, together with Stan and Bill Burchett. We are all getting on as well as can be expected and we finish our course in two weeks. (By the time you receive this I shall be on my way back to Moncton. After a couple of weeks there, the four

2

of in hope to be catching the boat back to good old England.) Then there are the other lads, Pete, Ron, Allen, & Ken who are on the course behind us. They should be finished in four weeks now for a bit of back news now old Derek Cribbles was killed when his of our lads collided. It was a great shock to everybody. I hope there will be no more accidents.

I haven't had time to show your letter to the boys yet as I've only just received it — however, in soon as I get to dinner I'll pass it to them. No doubt you will get a letter from them — I hope you are not continually changing your address otherwise our letters may not reach you.

Well, Don, I'm very glad indeed that you married Betty when you got back. I hope you will be very

3

happy together – and don't let anything get you down, pal. I cannot count the number of times Ernie has said to me – "I hope old Don got married when he arrived home". He'll be darned pleased to see your letter, I bet!

Don, you have my sincere sympathy regarding your trouble at home. It was a bad stroke of luck – I do hope that your folks have finally settled down again. I don't know what I should have done – had it happened at our home. I was relieved to read your P.S. that your sister and parents are safe. Please remember me to votre soeur, will you, old man, if she can remember me"!

So you think I may be a little disappointed when I get back home eh? Well Don, maybe you're right, I've heard other chaps say the same thing, but, boy! you know how we felt about it at Summerside. Well, I still feel

like that - I'm simply dying to see all the folks again.
Well, now for a little "gen". on events since I left
you at Moncton. I want to apologize for Ernie and
myself for not saying goodbye to you when we left. As
you probably know we were in such a hell of a hurry
getting packed and everything that we never had time
to get around to seeing you. Anyway, maybe I'll see you
some day in England - I hope so. Will you keep
writing? Maybe you had letter address your next letter
to Moncton. Jo continue, we had a wizard journey
down through Washington + New York and - few hours
in N.Y. then on again though W. Carolina and Florida -
Florida is wonderful. We had a few hours at Palm
Beach and Ralph a day in Miami. Gosh! did we ever
notice the temperature change. We left snow in Montreal

and by the time we were in Miami we were sweating blood!! Then came that horrible crossing on that dirty little tub. Gosh, pal I was just as bad as when we crossed to Canada. Ernie was just the same. It certainly was a rough trip. I'm dreading going back again for fear of loosing the rest of my stomach!!

My first impressions of the Bahamas were pretty good – the islands are most picturesque and of course the weather is perfect – sometimes a little too hot. Remember how I used to shiver in Summerside. Ha! Never again!! It was quite a novelty handling English money once again, although the paper money is different. Silly things such as four bob notes have been introduced here. The coins are the same as in England. The population is about 90% coloured and most of the natives speak

2

extra exertion I put in at G.R. It's much more interesting when the course is more practical! The time has gone very quickly and I don't seem to be able to realise that in a couple of weeks I'll be on my way again. All of us (that you knew at Summerside are on English postings so you can imagine how happy we are).

Nassau has one great disadvantage, Don, although it wouldn't have bothered you very much!! Here are very few white girls here, and those that are here, are promptly wolfed by those types who can support a few more rings on their sleeves than yours truly! But I don't bother with girls now. No sir, that can wait until I get back home. (Big of me!!!!)

We have had quite a lot of time off here, and we usually spend it at the beach, swimming and sunbathing. I am nearly the same colour as the bread boys, but I guess I shall have lost it all by the time I get home. Too bad!! I certainly hope that this effort reaches you, actually I cannot tell you much about — actually, I know why — I could write I would like to tell you. As I have me again. It'. (No,) I will be making certainly be glad can come home wishing you all the care of yourself.

Well, Don, I'm O.K. in this place, you see what this page said, by the time this reaches you, Ernie under the showers at Monaton, not this time, pal!!! But gosh, I'll when this course is over so that I'll to England. So for now, I'll close, very hard of luck, and take care of you all pal

          Fred

P.S. My sincere regards to Betty.

Dad said he was shifted about so much in the RAF that he was meeting different people all the time. His requesting a home posting instead of the Bahamas 'lost' him a number of good friends, and then those he knew who left Canada with him were lost when he had a week's compassionate leave when his home was bombed on his wedding day.

He never did hear whether Bart (the Technicolor man) survived the War. His friend Derek, the Argentinian, with whom he shared an apartment in New York, was killed in the Bahamas when two Liberators hit each other. Fred, with whom he also spent leave in New York, was posted out to the Far East and Dad had correspondence with him until the War's end. Then there was Ernie the man with whom Dad swopped postings – he too went out East on Liberators with Fred. Dad knows he survived the War because he was out and back at work before Dad lost touch with Fred.

Cyril, who Dad met first in Saskatoon and then later in Jerusalem was posted out to the Far East and found himself in Indo-China when the War ended often flying Japanese planes. He married a French girl in Saigon and later met up with Grandad after the War when the latter was on the Jury at the High Court in London and Cyril was Clerk of the Court.

Dad has not heard from any of them since the War but some of their letters make interesting reading so I thought I should include a sample.

23rd Sept, 1945

F/O GREEN F.G.
No 165947 R.A.F.
SECTION 6
CEYLON AIR FORCES

Hello Don,

SECURITY: THINK—BEFORE YOU WRITE

ON ACTIVE SERVICE

BY AIR MAIL

AIR LETTER

IF ANYTHING IS ENCLOSED THIS LETTER WILL BE SENT BY ORDINARY MAIL

THIS LETTER IS FOR THE USE OF H. M. FORCES ONLY

Written in .... (Language)

Sender's Rank ....

No. ....

Name ....

D.P.W. 51-9607

NEW ADDRESS HERE

To

REASON FOR REDIRECTION

NOTE
PLEASE INFORM YOUR CORRESPONDENT DATE OF YOUR CORRECT ADDRESS

SIGNATURE OF POSTAL CLERK

R.A.F. Postal Stamp.

R.A.F. Form 1674

N. P.—89°

Rec. 16¹²/45

29, Kings Head Hill,
Chingford. E4.
14-12-45

Dear Don,

Having lost contact with many of my old school friends I was agreeably surprised to hear from you, through your sister.

It seems a far cry from the days when our only worry was Matric. & whether we would win the House football etc. A lot of water has passed under the bridge since those days, & I am afraid I have not much to recount of my activity during the war years.

I have been a mere civilian due to my occupation, & my one claim to fame is that I volunteered for air crew duties, was accepted, and placed on deferred service. However, 18 months elapsed before I heard from the R.A.F. to tell me that owing to surplus requirements I would not be needed. As the only Service left open to volunteering was the Submarine Service I left it at that, & I reconciled myself to the monotony of civilian life.

I had heard that you were in the R.A.F. but did not know, until to-day, that you were married. To be in the R.A.F. is distinction enough, but to embrace matrimony holy or otherwise, is a courage of a higher order. However,

joking apart, please accept my congratulations on your marriage
however late they may be.

It was certainly grievous to hear of the loss of Bob Horne
and others, & it is hard to imagine that such vital
personalities are dead. If anyone enjoyed life it was
Bob, and words can not express the futility I feel when
I think of his death. The War has taken a heavy toll
of the lads in our year at school, and any reunion would
leave many an empty place.

Maybe we can arrange a rendez-vous during your leave,
and have a drink somewhere. I leave it entirely to you,
and you need be under no obligation to make a date
if you are pushed for time.

Please forgive note paper and scrawl. The scrawl, I
put down to "Ben" Leonard who, as you remember, made
us write copious notes at fantastic speeds.

All the best.

Alan Smith.

166149 F/O C.E.Lavender.

A.T.A.I.U. S.E.A.

c/o 5 B.P.U.

RAF INDIA

Tues.26th Feb.46.

Saigon. F.I.C.

Dear Don,

Please excuse my pranging a typewriter but I do find it a
fraction quicker than writing and as the Officer Commanding the Saigon
Detachment of Tech. Intelligence, I have'nt got too much time to waste.
Most of the Japanese equipment that we have examined has been classified
as being absolutely useless to us, and has been handed over to the
French who are badly off for equipment of any sort for their colonial
forces. At the moment the detachment is instructing the French
how to fly certain aircraft and giving them the gen on such things
as machine guns, cannons, engines and other equipment including met.
instruments. The Flight Lieut who was the actual tech. gen man on
the unit went off at Xmas for a holiday back in Calcutta (our base HQ)
went into hospital with amoebic dysentery and then decided it was
not worth his returning as we had already examined the bulk of the
Jap stuff. And then of course with the arrival of the French Forces
from Europe we have got this job on hand now.

Actually I don't mind the racket but the French are a bit
uppish about it all and they seem to consider the equipment we are
giving them is rightfully theirs. One French Commandant said to
me about a month back,

"The equipment was never yours to give us, after all this is

2

French Indo China and you found the stuff here when you came"

I got really annoyed at this and started telling him in my
best french that in that case he could teach his own men how
to operate the radar and radio sets we had handed over to them
and who the hell did he think had protected the French population
from the Annamites who were in revolt with Japanese backing, uuntil
the arrivak of Leclercs men two months later.

The Japs have a wonderful saying that they often say to us.
We beat the French and they have never beaten us, so why should
we have to w rk for them, the English beat us not them.

Sorry but, I intended to thank you for your letter in the
first paragraph but I got mislaid in the process -- thanks a lot
for the letter which arrived today and for the congratulations
on my engagement. I guess that paragraph in the local shook
quite a few people. They must wonder what the Lavender boys are
up to, first Charlie marrying an Aussie, and then young Cyril
getting himself engaged to a French popsie. I can imagine
them turning their eyes towards little Fred, now in Ireland
and their questioning minds searching for some sweet colleen.

I met this girl the second day I was in Phnom Penh
the Capital of Cambodia where I was leading the recce group
of the unit until I came back here shortly after Xmas to take
over the whole detachment. During the five months that I was
there I managed to see her every evening with the exception of
six, four of which I was away at some other drome working..

She is typically French looking, actually she is a Corsican
by extraction, small, quiet but a very willing mixer RAF Phnom
Penh consisted of 10 officers and 5 B.O.R's and the Wing Commander
i/c used to ask me to bring Andree to all the RAF parties and